The Big Book
Of Saban

COMPILED BY ALEX KIRBY

CONTENTS

1
STRATEGY & SITUATIONS

Q. Nick, the three BCS championship games you coached in here at Alabama, mostly you guys were in control in the fourth quarter. Obviously this one was a dogfight going into it and throughout you had to deal with a quarterback like Deshaun Watson. How hard was this National Championship?

SABAN: It was tough. It really was. I think offensively we did a nice job of -- we knew it would be a little big-little I call it in this game. They do a lot of pressuring, stunt linebackers. We knew that sometimes that they would give us some negative plays. I wasn't happy about the sacks. But I also knew that we would be able to make some big plays against them because of the way they played, and I think that was really big in this game.

We felt like we had to win special teams in this game. We thought, to be honest with you, that we could do a better job against their quarterback than what we did. He did a fantastic job in the game. We didn't cover as well as we're capable of, and we weren't able to handle him up front with our rushers, and I think they had 80-some plays, and we got tired probably in the second quarter, and once that happened, it was even worse.

You know, we like to play more man-to-man, but when you play against such an athletic quarterback and you're playing man-to-man, nobody is looking at the quarterback so that makes it tough, and when we did play zone tonight we didn't do a very good job, we didn't tackle very well, break on the ball like we needed to. He extended some plays and made some big plays, but the guy is a fantastic player.

I think when you play players like this, the whole team has to win. It's not just the defense stopping him, it's the offense doing what they need to do, making plays on special teams that you need to make.

And that's what we were able to do in this game, and didn't control him as well as we'd like, and obviously we thought that we could, at least in the end, milk the clock so they wouldn't score again, but 12 seconds onside kick, it was over.

On the performance following the rain delay and who helps keep Saban on his toes:

SABAN: When we were in the locker room, you can only go on what you see. We had told the players before, because we anticipated that this might happen. This is exactly how we were going to handle a rain delay, and they handled it well in the locker room. We had great focus, great attention to detail. We were going over everything like it was halftime. Everybody had the right eyes, the right look in their eye, and all that kind of thing.

Obviously, we didn't come out and play with the same kind of energy and intensity, which is probably difficult especially with the circumstances in the game as they were. And then when you take a shot as soon as you go out there and they had a kick-off return for a touchdown, we didn't respond to that very well either. So there was a combination of things. I'm responsible for it, I need to do a better job of it. If you have any ideas of what I can do to myself, I'd be glad to do it. I feel bad about it. Any time our team goes out there and I don't think they're playing the way they should, then I'm constantly searching for what I could've done better, what we could've done better to help put them in a better position.

Offense

On whether game manager is a negative connotation for a quarterback:

SABAN: To me, you can't be a good quarterback unless you are a good game manager. You have the ball in your hand every time, and you are making some kind of choice and decision what to do with it. Whether you hand it off, what play you hand it off on or where you throw it in the passing game. You have to process a lot of information quickly and make quick decisions. I don't think it's fair to AJ because I've said he's a really good game manager for us that it's like, that means he doesn't do anything. He does everything. I don't think you can be a good quarterback unless you are a really good game manager. That's the ultimate compliment to me. You have to have the ability to make plays, but we've certainly been able to make a few with our quarterback this year, and I think it's going to be important that we continue to be able to do that as well.

On the success of running the ball up the middle and if that helps open up the rest of the offense:

SABAN: You kind of sound like my wife now. She grumbles a lot when I go home because she says we run the ball up the middle. I think that direct runs, which some people may say run the ball up the middle, are a bad thing, but we package a lot of our plays and when we get the look that we want, our offensive line likes to be physical and aggressive, so our backs do a good job of running the ball inside. We made some explosive runs running the ball inside. We also run the ball fairly effectively on the perimeter, and I think it's a combination of those things that are important to do. We are trying to do the best we can do with the players we have, to feature their talents in terms of what we need to do to be successful. When we execute, we do a pretty good job and sometimes when we don't, we don't look so good doing it. I think it comes down to execution, whether it's inside run, outside run, play-action pass or a drop back pass, and I think all those things are really important.

On the amount of first-down pass plays and if it helps open up the running game:

SABAN: Well I think the balance is the most important thing. I think the best down to throw it on is first down. You usually know what you want to get, especially if you can run the ball. The other teams, probably 70 or 80 percent of the time, are in some kind of safety down, middle of the field, closed type of defense, which is the best time to throw it. I think we have to continue to mix it up, and try to keep the team off balance based on whether its formations, how we line up, and some of the packages that we put together based on what they line up in. That determines what we do, so some of that is called, and some of it is 'this is best thing to do against this particular situation.' We've been doing a good job with that. When I'm talking about game management, that's the kind of stuff that I'm really referring to.

On what teams have been doing to slow down the Alabama offense:

SABAN: I'm not sure it's always about what they did. When we watch the film, most of the time it is about what we did and in some cases what we didn't do. We need to execute better. We need to do things better. We need to get better play at every position. We need to play together better. We need to stay positive in what we try to do and get some trust and belief in each other, in that if everybody does the right things, we're going to have a chance to be successful. I said this at the press conference after the game, the way Ole Miss has tried to play us the last three years is putting everybody up in the box and dare you to throw the ball. We executed in the passing game at times and we did not execute like we need to at times. We left some plays on the field with dropped balls, missed throws, a couple of misreads, a couple of not-so-good routes and sometimes we could have had a little better pass protection. So I don't think it is any one specific thing, I think there are some things we need to do to execute better and that will help us.

On whether he is concerned that there have not been many big pass plays in the last few weeks:

SABAN: We want to make explosive plays. Florida played a lot of man-to-man in the game and we didn't separate well all the time and when we did separate we didn't make the throws. We probably need to stretch the field vertically a little bit more and continue to try to make big plays down field. We have some people who can do that and I think that's something that is important, but when we tried a couple in the last game they were covered, so we need to do a better job in separating. I think sometimes we get a little impatient and you can't do that when people are playing close coverage. You usually beat them, not down the field, but at the line or out of the break and you have to have a lot of patience and confidence to try to do that. I think our guys are playing with confidence, but sometimes I think when they get in close coverage, they get a little impatient.

On why Auburn's running game is so good:

SABAN: I think first of all their offensive line, they've got four guys that have played a lot of football and are all good players, and I think the offensive line is one of the strengths of their team. I think Ben Tate, as I have said before, is an outstanding running back. I think the multiples of presentation that you get from motions and personnel groups and those types of things, to run the same plays basically for them, sometimes they get the defensive players a little bit out of sorts. I think that one of things we want to make sure we're lined up properly and can try and fit the runs and do the best job we can to stop the run. They do a good job in the running game and they run power and counter and zone play and sweep and they've got a lot of complimentary reverses, misdirection plays and play passes off of that. When you load the box all the time, they eventually hit a play pass on you for a big play.

On passing game utilizing a number of players and taking what defense gives you:

SABAN: I think it's totally taking what the defense gives you. There is an old saying, if you take what the defense gives, they will eventually give you the game. So, if the people aren't open or they are dropping deep in zone and taking the vertical throws away and you drop the ball down to the check down and the guy gains six, eight 10 yards, that's a positive play. We have good guys and that's just another opportunity to get them the ball in space. I think the tight end is probably the best mismatched player on the field. I've always said that, in terms of who is covering him, where he lines up and how he gets defended. All these things are positives in my opinion. The quarterback makes good decisions and gets the ball in the right places and he's got the patience to do it and that's one of the reasons we have not turned it over a lot is we're not putting the ball where it shouldn't be going.

On philosophy of playing running backs during a game:

SABAN: I basically sort of get a feeling when the game's going on, we usually say we are going to have a guy carry it three or four times and the next guy is going to go in and carry it three or four times and then maybe you have a guy that is assigned to a specific role, whether its third down or whatever. Sort of from that scenario, you kind of get a feel for who has the hot hand or who maybe is the guy that's rolling out there like you would like to see it and maybe that guy plays a little bit more than the other guys in that particular game. It's really evaluate them and see who's got the feel.

On the depth at running back:

SABAN: I think I would always be comfortable having three guys. I also think that running back is a position where good special team players come from. If we have some other guys that have those qualifications, I certainly feel like we could take more. Roy Upchurch has been one of our best special teams players. Terry Grant became a very good special teams player for us last year. There are certain positions on the field -there are models in the NFL now, and I now Bill Belichick does this in New England, where a backup running back has to be able to contribute on special teams. A third down back, which may be your third back, has to be able to contribute on special teams, otherwise with a 47 man roster you don't have enough guys to play on special teams. In college you have more players, you can take more players, but there are still some positions that are better suited, body type and athletic ability wise, to play on special teams and running back would be one of those. I would like to have three good functional backs that can play in our offense at a minimum for the first game. We would like to have that.

On the role of the running game on the passing game:

SABAN: Balance is what you are always looking for on offense. We probably ran the ball a little bit better than what we anticipated what we might be able to in the game. That was the plan to run direct runs at them and looking at the film if we finished some blocks and done some things a little better we probably could have ran it more effectively. When you are running the ball you are creative positive down and distance situations for yourself offensively. The defense is out of balance and you are going to get more circumstances where the passing game can be a little easier to execute because you are not getting in those passing downs. I think it is a real critical factor.

Defense

On liking the nickel defense because it is flexible against different formations and personnel groups:

SABAN: When you play regular defense and you only have four defensive backs and when you play a three-four and you're symmetrical, you don't have problems in adjustment. As soon as you try to play over and under, you've either got to slide backers out on spread out formations, or you've got to walk somebody out because you only have four defensive backs. When you play nickel, you've already got a guy built in so that's how he makes his living being walked out on somebody and covering somebody outside the formation. You don't put a player who is not used to being in the position. It's easier to make adjustments because you've got five guys in the game instead of four, so you can have defensive backs on both edges, so no matter what they do, you are set. Now when they get in tight formations with a whole bunch of guys in the backfield, then you have a harder time getting eight-man fronts. That usually doesn't happen when they have three receivers in the game.

On defending a diverse running game:

SABAN: It takes a tremendous amount of discipline all around. You can't just play good gap control on the inside and fit the plays exactly like you're supposed to. The perimeter players need to do a good job as well. Probably as many good plays as they have are because of their perimeter plays. I think that's a real key. The way you play to stop the runs, you can't give up big-play passes, which we gave up a couple last year, and they've hit on numerous occasions this year against people. This takes a lot of discipline for everybody to exactly what they're supposed to do and be exactly where they're supposed to be because Auburn attacks the perimeter just as effectively as they do the interior, so every play you've got to be sound in both areas.

On using man-to-man or zone defense and how it's used to defend Auburn:

SABAN: It's very similar situation to the other running quarterbacks we've faced this year. They get in empty and you're trying to play man-to-man, or they free-release the back and the guy's got him. You run out of there and they run a quarterback draw or he scrambles with the ball and all of a sudden you've got four guys playing against five. You have to play a certain way so that you don't give opportunities to a great player. Newton recognizes it like that, and he knows exactly what he wants to do. It's difficult to defend so you've got to make sure that you've always got enough guys in there to stop them.

On what the defense was able to do last year to limit Ryan Mallet's effectiveness:

SABAN: Well I don't think what happened last year will have anything to do with what happens this year. First of all, I think we had a pretty good defensive team last year and made some plays in the game when we needed to make them. I think it will be a totally different challenge. I think they've got nine starters back on offense so they're better in terms of their consistency and execution. I think he's more comfortable in what he's doing and what he's expected to do, not that he wasn't a very good player last year, he certainly was. I think Bobby Petrino does a great job with him in terms of game plan, schemes and getting him in the right things so this will be a real challenge for this team this year, but also an opportunity for them to learn, grow, develop and try to get better.

On the risks and rewards of blitzing:

SABAN: I think any time you can affect the quarterback, and we haven't had a lot of sacks, but we have pressured him a lot, hit him a lot and pressured him in the pocket, which I think is really important.

The secondary gets affected when you rush four guys too. They've still got to cover somebody. You just might be covering with one less guy. I think it's just like pitching baseball. Sometimes you rush three guys, sometimes you rush four guys and sometimes you rush five or six and affect what they do. Most people who have one pitch in baseball; eventually they hit it - sometimes out of the park. That's kind of how we've always tried to play defense, in terms of how we present what we do in an aggressive style to try to dictate what the offense does, rather than always allowing them to dictate what we do. Does it create more multiples for the players? Absolutely, but it can be very effective if it's executed properly.

On what makes Alabama and Texas the top two defenses against the run:

SABAN: I don't really know why. First of all, I think they have good players and I think we have good players and it starts with that. I think in both cases those players are pretty well coached in terms of how they play in the scheme that they play and what they do and there are some similarities in the backgrounds and all that, but I don't think that's what makes it that way. I think it's the fact that they do a really good job of coaching their players. Will Muschamp does a really good job. I don't know everybody else on their staff and he's done that just about every place he's been and they have very good players. Their players play hard, they play with a lot of toughness and they play with a lot of discipline and doing what they're supposed to do, so the scheme works well for them.

There could be a totally different system and scheme that somebody ranks just as highly, or does just as well in, because they are coached well in that particular system and scheme and their players have the same qualities because they've responded to the things they need to do to play well as a unit. Their guys have and it's probably because it's the good job they've done, they have good players and those players play well together.

On the role of safeties when McCoy takes off and runs the ball:

SABAN: The safeties are not necessarily responsible for McCoy when he takes off with the ball. Everybody's got an assignment each time on defense. They run zone-option, where he pulls the ball sometimes. They run quarterback counters. They run quarterback draws. I think that the fact is they are such a good passing team and he's such a good passer and they have very good passing efficiency in all that they do. They are a very good third-down team. They force you to really try and play more where you are covering your receivers, so now you have less people in the box, which makes it more difficult to defend quarterback runs and I think that's one of the things that he has as much speed as any quarterback that we have played against all year. We are going to have to be more disciplined, especially up front in the front seven, of making sure that our eye control and our keying is very disciplined, so that we have the right guys in the right places when he decides to run the ball, because you are a little bit spread out with the kind of offense that they run.

On making a prolific offense like Arkansas throw the ball to beat you:

SABAN: No. When they get five times more yards throwing than they do running, you have to adapt and play a little bit more coverage and try and take away what they do best. I think there is a balance in all that. I don't think you can compromise and just not be sound against the run and not have all the gaps, because they have two good runners now and if you do that they are going to come out of the gate on you and they are good space players. I think you have to play the situations in the game, but I also do think that you do have to emphasize coverage and be able to play the passes, especially so that you don't give up big plays. I think the last game they played; both sides had lots of big plays. If you give up big plays, there are a lot of stats in the NFL that talk about how many explosive plays in every drive and if you get one then your chance of scoring goes up big time and if you get two, your chance almost doubles. When you give up those big plays, just like when North Texas scored on us, they had two big plays in the drive. I don't care who was out there playing, you can't give them up. It's going to be important for us to continue to get explosive plays, but not to give them up and you do have to play a little bit different. You can't play run down defense, when you think the team is going to throw it.

On the front seven and their importance this week against Arkansas:

SABAN: I think it's a big key. I don't think you can commit people to extra rushers all the time to try and get pressure on the quarterback to try and affect the quarterback because you are going to be thinner in the back end, in terms of your coverage. So to be able to get pressure with four guys rushing is really important. I didn't think we did a very good job of that last year in the game we played last year against them. I think it's going to be really important that we can do that in this particular game. So, I think having good pressures is also important. I think having coverages and I think doing multiples of things that change it up a little bit. Playing defense is a lot like being a pitcher. If you're a one-pitch guy, they are probably eventually going to hit you. If you've got good blitzes and you blitz all the time, eventually you're going to live by the sword and die by the sword.

But if you've got a good changeup and you throw a slider on the outside. I saw this guy the other day, they were talking about all he does is throw a fastball up in the strike zone and changeup down in the strike zone and they guy is winning lots of games. I forget the guy's name or who he pitches for. In playing defense, especially when you're playing against a real good quarterback, is a lot like that. If he knows what you're doing all the time before he gets the ball in his hands, he's going to be able to make a good decision and take advantage of it. So, you've got to be able to pitch a little bit.

On Justin Woodall and his ability to call the defensive signals:

SABAN: Well I think that is certainly a responsibility in the secondary and Justin has been a starter for us all last year and certainly did an outstanding job for us. I think you get into a little bit of a comfort zone as a player when you have somebody like Rashad Johnson, who is very bright and a leader and actually wants to take the responsibility of making the calls and understanding things because that's his personality type and he has those types of leadership skills. I think that one of things that we've sort of tried to pass the torch to Justin, because he has the most experience at safety is for him to contribute to that, but I do think it is important that both safeties communicate that. I think it's going to be important for Mark Barron to continue to grow in that area. Communication is critical in the secondary.

Even if you communicate the wrong thing, if everybody does it wrong, its right. Does that make sense?

It sounds backwards. If we are supposed to be playing cover two and everybody plays cover three we're fine. We can get mad on the sideline and throw our headsets because someone missed a check, but we're not going to give up a touchdown. We are still playing sound. Everybody is playing the same thing. It might not be what we wanted to play. The problem in the secondary is when you're supposed to be playing cover three and these guys on this side are playing cover three and the guys are on this side are playing cover two then somebody runs down the middle of the field and there is nobody there.

That's the reason that communication is so important. The safeties must communicate with the corners and they must communicate to the perimeters, the outside backers, what the support is as well as the coverage we are playing. I think both safeties communication is critical and Justin has to assume some of that role.

On what will become of the Jack Linebacker position with the absence of Brandon Fanney:

SABAN: Well, we have lots of Jack linebackers. We had one in the spring. Fanney didn't participate in spring practice and we didn't drop football at Alabama. We still had football. One player can't make our team one way or the other. We have other players that we'll try at that position - Eryk Anders has done a good job. We'll take every linebacker we have on the team, inside or out, and try to make sure that we get the best four linebackers on the field, relative to their strengths and how they can help our team. That's two inside guys and two outside guys.

Last year when we went into camp, we only had one linebacker that had ever played. Rolando McClain was the only linebacker that had any experience that had ever played. We moved Reamer from inside linebacker to outside, Hightower was a freshman, Fanney was a defensive end that we moved to outside linebacker, so that's how we got where we were. Maybe after eight or ten practices, maybe after two weeks of practices, maybe after 20 practices, at some point in time if some combination of guys looks like it's going to be best for our team, then that's when we'll make a choice and decision about that. But I think we have some good players and I think we have some good candidates. I think there is lots of opportunity there for lots of players.

On the play of Terrence Cody and Alabama holding Clemson to zero rushing yards:

SABAN: They didn't really have zero rushing yards in the game. That is the one thing about college football that is a little messed up. They had 30 yards rushing in the game. That is the running plays when they ran the ball. The sacks should come off the passing yardage like it does in the NFL. So they had 30 yards rushing in my mind. They lost 30 yards passing because of sacks. They could have had 100 yards rushing but if they had a lot of sacks they could have had no yards rushing. I think two things contributed to that. I think everyone up front did a good job and Terrence certainly did his job well and was a factor in the game in the middle. We made good adjustments to their formations, we didn't get out-flanked and we did a good job on the line of scrimmage with our front people and out linebackers. That was a real key to being able to stop the run.

The second thing was the way the game went and we got ahead a little bit they aborted the run some. Because we stopped them on the run we created more positive down and distance situations for the defense and we were able to play what we wanted to play. It was not our plan to pressure them a lot because of all the screens they threw. They throw a lot in games and that is a way to give up big plays when you apply a lot of pressure and they throw a wide receiver screens. We did pressure several times in the game and did get pressure but all the sacks came off of a four-man rush.

Q. When you're facing a quarterback that doesn't have much experience, how do you try to take advantage of that? At the same time with an inexperienced quarterback this year, how do you try to guide him through games until he gets that experience?

SABAN: Well, you know, I think that everyone develops at a little different pace and rate, depending on their ability to learn the knowledge and experience, how they learn from their lessons. And I think specifically in our case Greg McElroy learns very quickly and has had some experience. But I also understand that until he makes plays in the game, he's not gonna fully have, you know, the trust and respect of all of his teammates, even though they really, really like him and they really like him as a leader.

I think the biggest mistake you can make in development of any new player, young player, inexperienced player, is give him too many things to do, and increase the multiples of the kind of mental errors that they can make.

I think that it depends, from a defensive perspective, who the guy is that you're trying to defend. If he's a smart guy, if you try to pressure him, you may enhance his chances of making plays because he understands it, he sees it, and his reads actually become a little easier.

If you try to play all coverage against him and don't pressure him and he's a good runner, he may hurt you with his feet.

So I think to really answer that question effectively, you'd have to know the specifics of who you were trying to defend.

Q. Tim Tebow, the passer and Tim Tebow the rusher, how do you balance that game defensively?

SABAN: It's very difficult, because Tim Tebow is a fantastic football player and he's a big, strong runner, which most of the time you don't play a quarterback that has those sort of big tailback attributes as a runner.

And he's a very efficient passer. I mean, they're one of the top passing efficiency teams in the country. And that always starts with the quarterback who is completing 66 percent.

And they do a good job of spreading you out, making you defend the whole field and enhancing his chances when you're spread out of being able to scramble and make plays as well as scramble and make plays thrown.

So it's a very, very difficult preparation, and I think that he contributes largely to that because of the style of player he is and the great physical attributes that he has as a runner and as a passer. And he's a very instinctive guy. So he doesn't make a lot of bad choices as a quarterback. And that's why they have such good efficiency and balance in their offense.

On his simple answer to why Alabama is able to keep teams from scoring large amounts of points:

SABAN: The simple answer is that we have pretty good players that play well together and execute the scheme. Everyone does their job and that gives us the best opportunity to be successful. I don't know what else to say besides that. I can't really speak for everybody else. I don't get to see a lot of the other games. I don't really know what is happening. I don't know what other people's personnel are. I don't know what they are trying to do. I really don't know what they are having to play and defend against, but probably a common denominator in all of that is a lot of mental errors, a lot of missed tackles. Those two things usually lead to a lot of bad stuff happening when you don't play good defense.

On being aware of unconventional offensive plays:

SABAN: I think, first of all, Gus Malzahn does a great job with their offense, and they've been very, very productive. And he does a very good job of utilizing the players that they have, and roles that they can be productive in. But they have a lot of, whatever you want to call them, gadget, trick plays, crazy formations, whatever you want to call it. And I think the big things is, you got to get your players on defense settled enough to change personnel, when they're going at a fast pace. They're doing a lot of things that can disrupt defensive players, and I think the most important thing is that you get lined up and you can play and the players are confident in what they're playing, and they're not all running around trying to get lined up and making adjustments that are going to put them in a bad position.

Special Teams

On searching for the right 11 on the kickoff team:

SABAN: I think that we had some guys that did extremely well on kickoff coverage. We had four or five guys that really did a good job. We had a couple other guys that did an okay job. Then we had a couple guys that probably didn't do it quite the way we would like for it to be done, and I think those guys have an opportunity to step up their game a little. We also have an opportunity to look at other people that might help them step it up, but that's that way at every position. Just because you played last week doesn't mean you are entitled to play this week. I think somebody told me there were like 30 former pro bowl players that got cut this past weekend or something. Is that right or wrong? I can't justify or verify that statistic, so I'm not trying to get quoted but how does that happen? How does that happen?

On whether or not a kicker who can tackle (Cade Foster) is assigned a lane on kickoff coverage:

SABAN: No, he's a safety. He has a responsibility to leverage the ball, relative to the rest of the kick coverage group. Cade was a linebacker in high school. He is a football player, is very aggressive and he has made several tackles on kickoff coverage, and that's a benefit because that's an area that we need to improve on. I think we're better than we were at this time last year in kickoff coverage but still not as effective as we need to be.

On the combination of good punter and punt returner:

SABAN: I've often said if you accumulate 100 yards of field position, no matter how you get it, usually equates in to six points. Obviously when we have 100 yards in punt returns and out net punting is minimized because of good punting, good coverage and good protection, I think P.J.'s only really had one not so good punt all year and that was in the last game on his first one. Other that, he has been really consistent and we've had good coverage. Our net punt had been an advantage to us, relative to how we have been able to return the ball on other people and how that changes field position. In the last game, we negated, I don't know, 60, 70, 80 yards in returns by penalties. Whether they were good penalties or bad penalties, they were still penalties that got called and we lost a lot of field position because of that, even though we were still successful in averaging over a first down on punt returns.

Q. Everybody is always going to remember this game (Clemson vs Alabama) and talk about this onside kick because it was so unexpected. Do you see that, though, as a reflection of how well-prepared you were to take the risk in that situation?

SABAN: Well, I think it's a calculated risk when you do something like that, but I think it's calculated based on your ability to execute relative to what the other team is sort of giving you. I think I spoke about this last evening, that you always have fakes in all these areas, and you always have special plays that you might use in certain situations. I think the thing that we look for as the game progresses, are they actually giving us that look that this might have the best opportunity to be effective in. We felt like that was the case last night. I felt like I think the score was 24-24 or something like that when we did it, that we actually needed to change the momentum of the game a little bit.

They sort of controlled the third quarter a little bit on us, and it certainly, because it worked and it was well-executed, it was a great kick by Griff, it was a good job by Marlon, to do it exactly like we drew it up, and we scored on a big play, I think, right after that, and I think that changed the momentum of the game and we got ahead in the game which allowed us to play a little differently because we weren't playing great on defense, and obviously Deshaun Watson is a fantastic player, probably had as big an impact on the game as any single player in the game. So to get ahead I think when you're playing against a player like that is really, really important, and I think it helped us change the momentum of the game.

The Option

Q. Although Florida does so many things offensively, it seems to be really adept at running the option right now. Could you comment just maybe on the difficulty of defending Florida's option?

SABAN: I think that what you say is very true. I think that to probably summarize their offense, they have a quarterback who can run the ball. They have some very good running backs who have great speed on the perimeter. And they are reading their plays almost each and every play as to whether they hand the ball off or option the ball, or even create a pitchman sometimes to option the ball.

Or even when they run a shuffle pass sometimes they have the option to pitch the ball. So that in itself is an option.

And so it is difficult to defend, because it's about numbers. So you really have an offense that the point of attack can change from out there to out here, to running it in here or throwing it down there. And that's about -- and all those things can change in one step, whether it's play action pass or how they create their options.

And the fact that they have a quarterback who is unique in terms of his ability to run the ball, execute their offense and be a very efficient, effective passer, makes it very important to play very disciplined team defense in terms of everybody keying, being in the right spot and making sure you keep the right side boards on the defense and they do it out of a lot of different personnel groups and different formations that so that makes it even more difficult for the defense to adjust to each one of those things correctly.

On the last time he faced a primarily triple-option football team:

SABAN: It has been a long time. We played Army when they used to run the wishbone when I was at Michigan State as a defensive coordinator in the '80s. We played Navy when I was a head coach at

Toledo - that might be the last time. But we did a lot of research, and a lot of work and a lot of study on these guys in the offseason, because we knew they were going to be one of the most different teams that we played. Actually it will be challenging for the players, probably, to do something different, to be honest with you. I know it's challenging to me as a coach to try to figure out, take some of the principles of things that you've done long ago and I'll try to have to reinvent the wheel. They give you a lot of formation multiples, which makes it a little harder to adjust. They do a really good job of executing what they do. It takes a lot of discipline on defense for everybody to do what they're supposed to do.

On what the preparation will be like for defensive signal callers:

I think it is for everybody. I don't think you can play - you don't really end up playing conventional type coverages. They're not conventional plays that you're going to see. In terms of, when I say 'conventional,' I don't mean that in a disrespectful way. I guess 'conventional' is all that you're used to. So it's going to be a lot of preparation for the entire defense. How you play the blocks. Who takes what on the option up front, how the linebackers in the front fits together, but then how the secondary rotates, and where the run-force comes from, and the discipline you got to have on the edges when they get the ball outside and pitch the ball. They make some big plays sometimes handing the ball off to the fullback, but they make a lot of big plays on the perimeter pitching the ball where somebody breaks down and run out of guys.

Red Zone

On importance of red zone and struggles both teams have had this year:

SABAN: I think there is good and bad in the red zone. You did something to get it down there. You can start with that, but you also want to finish when you get there and maximize the number of points that you get. They move the ball effectively and have gotten down there, which I think it's a credit to their offensive team. I think it's critical that last year the difference in the game was they scored when they got it in the red zone. I think they scored three out of four times, or maybe four out of five times, but I'm talking about touchdowns. We didn't always do that and it's going to be a critical part of the game as to who can finish in the red zone. The multiples add up between seven and three. In close games it always comes down to how efficient and effective you were on both sides of the ball. Did you get them stopped and were you able to convert and finish.

On whether red zone play is a point of emphasis early in camp or after the teaching/instructional phase:

SABAN: We have a teaching progression that we go through. The things we do in the red zone will probably require some fundamental teaching of three or four practice days before the players are ready to take that on in the progression of how they learn fronts and coverages on defense, as well as formations and plays on offense, because you do adjust what you do in the red zone because of depth of the field. One thing I will say is, defensively, this is the first time in the three years that we've been here that we've been able to accomplish our goal defensively in how we played in the red zone, and it was probably a real key in us being successful last year and being difficult to score on. If you don't give up big plays and you play well in the red zone, then all of a sudden you can get pretty difficult to score on. I think that was one of the key components to last year's team being successful and difficult to score on.

On opponents getting so many red zone opportunities even though the defense has stood strong:

SABAN: I think that playing in the red zone is a really important part of being a good defensive team. I think there are a combination of things that make you a good defensive team. Most of the time when you don't give up big plays, you play well in the red zone and you get pretty hard to score on. We've probably given up a few too many big plays. I don't know what the average number of opportunities for a team to be in the red zone at this point in the season would be, we've played five times and our opponents have been down there 14 times, I don't think that is too many but I don't really know. The key thing is when you get there you have to play the next play. Our guys have competed very well down there. You have to give them credit for the tenacity that they have. Would we rather have played and never let a team get down there? Sure. But we were better in the red zone last year and I think that contributed to our success and that is something that we have emphasized this year with this team and it is certainly something that has been good for us so far. The turnovers in the red zone and the big plays are probably the things that we need to continue to work and improve on.

The Spread Offense

Q. Talk about the impact of the spread offense on defenses in college football.

SABAN: Well, I just think that it's very difficult to defend. I think when the quarterback's a runner, you create another blocker, or a receiver that you have to cover. So that kind of creates another gap on defense. And I think that that's very difficult to defend.

But I think it's like anything else: the multiples of what you have to defend are what make it more difficult to defensive players. Just like in the old days when they used to run the wishbone. When you had to play against the wishbone, that was really different. So it was difficult to get the picture and look of what you needed to do to get your team prepared to be able to play against it.

I think to some degree the spread offense is the same way. A no-huddle offense is the same way. How do you get a scout team in practice to be a no-huddle team to get any kind of execution so that the defensive players start to develop the mentality they need to be able to change their routine and play without a huddle?

So I think the concept of the spread offense is outstanding because it makes the quarterback an 11th gap on defense, I always say. If you only had to defend that all the time, I think we could all get a little better at it. It's the multiple of the different things you see throughout the season that make it more difficult.

Q. As many teams are using the spread, do you see many teams in perhaps taking advantage of what you do and mimicking some of what you do? What advantage does that give you on the recruiting trail when you're recruiting offensive athletes who can play in a set like they would eventually play in the NFL?

SABAN: You know, I think one of the things we always tell

players when we're recruiting them is, you know, when you go to college, you're in the business of developing two careers. You want to develop a career off the field by graduating from school, and that's the most important career that you have to develop when you go to college. But you also want to have a great college experience as a football player, win a championship, be as good as you can be, and see if you can develop a career as a football player and play at the next level.

Being a little bit of a pro background guy, we've always tried to sort of pattern our systems out of how we could best develop guys to be able to do that. That's probably why we play offense the way we play it, and it's the way we play -- why we play defense the way we play it. And even special teams, we haven't gone to the spread punt, all that stuff, which is pretty predominant in college football.

I think there is some concerns at the next level, which is not our concern in college. I will say this: the spread offense, some of the things that are being done offensively in college football, is very challenging and very difficult to defend, especially if you have the kind of personnel to do that. So this is in no way a criticism of that style of offense, because I think it's very difficult to defend.

But I do think it's more difficult for the people in the NFL, which is really not our issue as college coaches, to sometimes evaluate players, a left tackle that never gets in a three-point stance, a quarterback who never takes a snap from under center, a runner that never gets the ball with his shoulders pointed down parallel to the line of scrimmage. Some of those things are evaluation issues, which it's the player's choice when he chooses that, where he wants to go to college, the style of offense or defense he wants to play.

Q. Nick, is it okay to have a 'game manager,' a quarterback? What does that term mean to you? Is that necessarily a negative when you throw that label out there?

SABAN: No, I think it's a part of the quarterback's job. I think when you manage the game, you make all the people on the offensive field feel like you're in command and you're in control in terms of the direction, how you call plays, the cadence, how you lead the team. And I think those things are an important quality in any quarterback.

So regardless of your talent level, and I think that because you distribute the ball every play as a quarterback, it's important that your decision making and judgment is good, and that you actually do a good job of managing how you distribute the ball, which is a critical factor in playing winning football.

Q. Nick, in this era of all these spread offenses and quarterback-centric offenses, what do you make of two teams that run the ball and play physical and have defenses, run-stopping defenses being in this game and being the two teams left?

SABAN: I think it speaks a lot for whether we call it old-fashioned football or whatever; that if you're big, if you're physical, you win on the line of scrimmage, even though both teams are capable of making explosive plays throwing the ball and you control the line of scrimmage on the defensive side of it, that you've got a really good opportunity to win.

And I think these two teams that are in this game this year kind of proved that in terms of the style and nature of play. And I think when you can do those things, you can play-- you have a better chance to play more consistently by having good defense and being able to have balance on offense, and offensive system that allows you to do that.

So maybe that's why these teams could play with a little bit more consistency.

On difference between Florida's offense from 2008 to 2009:

SABAN: I don't think there is a whole lot of difference, other than the way they probably utilize their personnel. Their personnel groupings are a little bit different because they are getting two or three in there now instead of Percy Harvin being the guy that joined those guys in the backfield last year a lot. They do a lot of the same things; they just put them in there and do it. That doesn't make it any easier to defend. So, I would say conceptually, they run the same plays. They always give you a lot of multiples in formations and adjustments. They get in a lot of empty and reload. They do a lot of the things they did a year ago, I think the way they present it is a little bit different. Last year, they hardly ever got in regular, just regular two back, tight end and two receivers, they do that on occasion this year. I think it's all a function of utilizing the personnel that they have. It's not really conceptually changing the philosophy of what they do on offense.

On the progress your defense has made against the spread offense since last year:

SABAN: I think we played fairly well against these guys last year for three quarters of the game and didn't get things done in the fourth quarter like we needed to. We didn't make some plays on critical third downs, especially in the red zone that they were able to convert into touchdowns on three occasions. We've probably played against more of that type of stuff and I think that hopefully we understand what we need to do better, but it's still when they spread you out it comes down to the personnel mismatches that they create and how your players respond to what they need to do to try and get them covered. Sometimes when you get these guys covered, Tebow takes off running with the ball, which is another issue and problem you have to try and solve defensively because not only do you have to play pass defense, but you have to worry about him running for a first down as well.

On similarities to Florida's offense and Mississippi State's offense:

SABAN: I think it's changed relative to the personnel that he has. I think the core, the philosophy, the zone dive, zone option, counter plays and quarterback reads are the same. They also have Chris Relf that they use more as a running quarterback when they put him in there. Tyson Lee can run the ball. He makes yards running it. He is a great competitor, does a very good job of executing their offense and does a good job of reading for them. I think philosophically they are the same. I think the way they utilize their personnel is a little bit different.

On defending the spread, is the nickel back look almost the base defense now?

SABAN: Well, I think every team goes about it a little bit differently. I think some teams still play the spread with regular people. We can do it both ways and we always make a decision on how we feel like we can adjust best to what they do, relative to the players that we have. The most difficult thing in regular people, depending on your system and scheme, is not the basic formations, but how you adjust to all the other formations.

It's a lot easier when you're in nickel and have five defensive backs to adjust to formations like multiples, empty, four wide outs and those types of things and not get linebacker-type guys spread out in space where they are not used to playing. We always have to make those decisions based on those types of things. When you play a really good running team like this team, there is certainly a consideration to just leaving your big guys in there and just playing with them.

On coaching against an offense like Urban Meyer's Florida Offense:

SABAN: I think they are a spread offense. Obviously the quarterback is a unique player, in terms of his ability to throw the ball and be a very good runner, and that always creates one more blocker and one more thing that you have to defend. We have seen some parts of what they do throughout the year, so we have some frame of reference of what they do. I think the biggest thing they do is utilize a lot of different formations, a lot of different personnel groups and utilize their players in different ways.

They have a lot of good players and that makes it very challenging to try and stay in the right leverage positions and make the adjustments you need to make so that you're not unsound, in terms of something that they do. Their offensive line, in the meantime, has done a pretty good job of blocking the upfront people. So it's really important to control your gaps up front and play on the line of scrimmage, be aggressive, get off your blocks and make plays. They are reading a lot of the things that they do so as defensive player you have to read and react to what they are doing as well.

Q. I think the other day you mentioned that the Gators had 162 different formations alone. I was just wondering how that compares to other teams in terms of how much you have to prepare that way and how that compares to your team?

SABAN: Well, I would think that those are quite a few more multiples than what you would typically see. And what we would typically see and probably quite a few more multiples than our offensive team would be presented or we would present ourselves when we do our own self-scout.

And I think the reason I said that was trying to make a point of the problems that their offense creates in terms of how they use their personnel and the multiples that they use that personnel in.

They don't even run 162 different plays, but it's the way they present the plays to confuse the defensive players that is the point I was trying to make.

The Wildcat

On the Wildcat formation:

SABAN: We're fortunate to have a couple of really good runners. The offensive line does a really good job. I think you're adding a gap to the defense when you do this because somebody has to cover the quarterback. Even though he's not going to get the ball, somebody has to cover him. Therefore you create a little bit of a running advantage for yourself, even though they know what's coming. That's been a very effective tool for us in the last two years. Hopefully we'll be able to continue to execute it and get the kind of production that is helpful to our offense. It also makes the other team have to prepare for it and spend time on it, as well as all the other things that you do.

On the wildcat offense and using a quarterback in that role like Auburn does:

SABAN: I think anytime they have a quarterback running it, it does affect how you play it because there is the potential of the guy being able to throw the ball. I think sometimes when a quarterback is not playing it, Darren McFadden threw it some. I think it takes a lot of discipline and eye control that no matter how you play it, everybody's got to key in on what they are supposed to do. If you've got a guy man-to-man and you're playing him man-to-man, then you better watch him and look at him and cover him. They did hit Ole Miss for a touchdown pass out of that because the guy wasn't looking at his man, they had him man-to-man. I think discipline and eye control, you know there is a picture when we come out of the locker room that's got Bear Bryant's picture on it and there is something about discipline and eye control on there that I read every time I walk out. I think that's important in every part of football, but especially important in wildcat.

On wildcat offense as compliment to your offensive package:

SABAN: I think it needs to be a compliment to what you do, and I think one of the reasons we've done it more is we've had a reasonable amount of success doing it. I think every team will probably play it a little bit different and you never know for sure how they are going to play it until you get in the game. I think that has something to do with how much you use it too.

On why the wildcat offense is a tough adjustment for defenses:

SABAN: I think that, we saw it in the NFL last year. I think when people see something that is new and difficult to defend, which it is, because you create another gap on defense. The quarterback is no longer the quarterback. If none of the coverages that we play and if we play man-to-man, nobody has the quarterback. Now you put him out as a receiver and put a tailback in there, you have created another gap to defend on defense to run the same plays that you normally run. By using the motion gaps or speed sweeps, at least keeps the people on the perimeter honest. Everybody is developing their ways to try and defend this, but I also think people are expanding what they do in this, more and more, that if you're not defending the middle of the field properly, they are going to have some things they can do to take advantage of that. Ole Miss has always been able to do that. They could do it at Arkansas.

Up-Tempo Offense

Q. The speed of the game is obviously a subject you'd trust in your opening statement. With that offense being sped up so much, how much has that altered your philosophy on what you do on the defensive side of the football?

SABAN: I think it's affected it tremendously. Being an old NFL guy, the way you play defense in the NFL is you play a lot of specialty defense because everything is based on situations. What pace of play has done to the college game does not allow to you do that. So you have to basically play the same players in every situation because, if you do play situation defense and you're allowed to sub in that particular situation, you can't get the players out of the game. So it affects how you recruit. You can't recruit as many specialty players. And you have to be able to match up in all circumstances and situations with teams that actually play that way, which is more difficult. I don't think there's any question about the fact that it's more difficult to play defense, and I think that's why you see more points being scored, and I don't think that trend's going to change any time soon.

Q. A few years ago you were very passionate about your dislike for no-huddle offenses because of concerns about safety for players and fatigue. The past couple years you have kind of changed. You hired Lane, kind of changed your offense. How difficult is that for you to make the decision to kind of go somewhat in a different direction but still incorporate some of the things that you do?

SABAN: I think, first of all, Lane was really a no-huddle guy. That was something that we did philosophically because of the issues that it created for us, you know, defensively. And it was the rule. You know, just like I don't necessarily agree with the illegal man down field rule and a guy should be able to go seven yards down field on a pass play. I don't agree with that. But it is a part of our game. It is the rule.

So, for us to not use those plays is a disadvantage for us. All right. So even though we may not philosophically agree that this is the way football was meant to be played or should be played, if it creates issues for the other team and for the defense, and pace of play has been something that I think has done that, so have all of these run pass option plays that people run, then we need to use those things, too, or we're creating a disadvantage for ourselves.

It's been a work in progress for us to learn how to do that because we do not have an offensive coach on our staff that came from that background, came from that hurry-up, no-huddle offense. I think our coaching staff, including Lane, has done a fantastic job sort of developing a system that has been very effective for us in terms of what we've been able to do.

So it's the issues and problems that it creates that made us move in that direction, and that's what we will continue to do.

On the advantages/disadvantages of speeding up the offensive tempo:

SABAN: We just seem like we've played better, that's the only advantage that I can say. We've always sort of practiced a lot of no huddle. We've always thought it was a good thing to set the tempo, but it seems to help us with our tempo on offense. We seem to play fast and get going a little bit better when we set the tempo, so that has been the advantage. I don't know what the disadvantage is because we haven't really made a lot of errors, it hasn't affected our execution. We've actually played better when we've played sped up.

2
COACHING

Q. Last night on your radio show you said at some point you have to take the game. What exactly did you mean by that? And how do you go about doing that?

SABAN: Well, I just think that when you play in games like this, there's always sort of a turning point in the game. First of all, you expect two good teams playing, it's going to be a close game. There's going to be some situation in the game where you need to make a play or they might need to make a play that's going to make the difference in the game. And your ability to rise up in those situations and be able to do that, whether it's critical 3rd down to maintain possession of the ball on a scoring drive, or whether it's a defensive stop, whatever it might be, you know, you have to be ready to execute in those kinds of situations in the game. And there's going to be some point in the game where that particular circumstance and situation probably will have an impact on the outcome of the game. And your ability to successfully execute in those kinds of situations I think is critical when you play in games like this.

Q. Two of the more emotional people last night we talked to after the game, AJ McCarron and Jim McElwain, and AJ said he thought that McElwain let the reins off him a little bit, let him loose, only because McElwain couldn't get in trouble from you because McElwain is leaving town. Your thoughts on what that win meant to AJ and to Jim?

SABAN: First of all, it was our plan to do what we did. It's something that we wanted to do more of in the first game. And, look, I think it's important that whoever is calling the plays, whoever is calling the defenses, whoever is making the special teams calls, you gotta trust the players.

And if you're afraid to do things because you don't trust the players, then you're probably never going to be able to allow them to grow and be all that they can be. It's just like your children. There's just some things you have to let them do. You can't protect them all the time.

And I think that's what AJ sort of proved to all of us. And I'm not talking about Jim McElwain here. That if we were going to be able to have success against a defensive team like LSU, which is a very good defensive team, we're going to have to throw the ball, we're going to have to trust the quarterback to do it.

And my statement is: Look at it this way. If we don't do it, we can't win. So we need to do it. If the guy plays well, we'll have an excellent chance in moving the ball. And if he doesn't play well, we probably won't have much of a chance to be successful offensively. But if we don't do it, we may not have a chance either.

And I think Jim sort of felt the same way about that and did a great job of implementing what he did in letting AJ do what we needed to do in this particular game to be successful.

I just want everybody to know I'm not conservative. I want to throw the ball all the time. The interception we threw in the first game, I said: Throw the ball on first down. I wanted to throw the ball on first down in that game because of the way they play.

And we didn't do it enough. But I think we learned in the first game that's what we needed to do to be successful against the style of play and the good football players that they have on their defensive team. They're a good secondary. But they put pressure on their secondary and they have a very good front.

And everybody on our team did a good job. We protected well. Receivers caught the ball well. AJ made good choices and decisions about how he distributed the ball, and I think that's why we had success offensively.

But if we didn't win that game and LSU scored points, everybody would be saying why didn't we score more touchdowns. We tried seven field goals and made five.

Q. Were Ole Miss able to stop a flukey play against Arkansas, they might be here instead of your team. Does that illustrate how difficult it is to win and maybe your program -- people think it's easy and maybe is it really harder than what a lot of people think, considering the success you guys have had?

SABAN: Well, it certainly isn't easy and it's not easy for anybody in the organization. It's not easy for the players. These guys do a lot of hard work, work a lot of long hours. The players practice -- and these are players, these are college students, and that's something that people overlook and realize. They have tests. We have finals week next week. We have an 86 percent graduation rate, so we expect our guys to do those things the right way. That takes a lot of time. Most of you probably were students at some point in time and probably understand that.

And so it's not easy at all, and it's not easy to -- consistency and performance define success. It's not easy to deal with success. It's not easy to deal with failure. So to have the right psychological disposition to be able to sustain all those ups and downs and look at every one of those challenges as a test, not a sign of what's going to happen; it's a test of how you respond to it, how you react to it and how you try to take advantage of it, good or bad. That's the only way you have a chance.

And to get young people to really understand that, buy into it, have the maturity to sustain it throughout a season is very, very difficult. And I have a lot of respect for the way people compete, the way they play, how hard their players play, and not just did they win or lose. And you're right, we are fortunate that the ball bounced -- our team did everything they can do in terms of how they responded the rest of the season, and you know, when we lost a game early, we didn't control our own destiny. So somebody else helped us.

Q. Kind of staying with that thought, is that one of the most satisfying aspects of your job in coaching college athletes is rebuilding teams year after year, teaching them and seeing them get it?

SABAN: Well, that's always the goal, but still, it's all about how you finish. I mean, I'm very proud of what our team has accomplished to this point in the season, but the legacy of the team really is about how they finish the season. And really, how you've taught those lessons, a part of that is how you finish the season, too.

So you know, when we look at the cut-up some day down the road, are we going to see their guys playing their best when their best is needed, which is in championship games; and this is certainly a Championship Game. That's the challenge that we have. And it's self-gratifying to see, but it's disappointing when you can't come through for your players to help them do that when they need you the most.

Q. How has Lane Kiffin improved you as a coach?

SABAN: I think that everyone on our staff, I think we all try to improve each other. I think every new coach that you bring to your staff, when you bring them, brings positive energy, new ideas, new enthusiasm.

So, I think every coach that we brought in has made an improvement in terms of helping me develop new ideas, new experiences, because we're always all looking for a better way.

And I think all of the coaches on our staff have done very well when it comes to that responsibility of looking for a better way and doing a good job. And I think, you know, coaches do a good job in a lot of ways. You know, if they are coordinators, are they good play callers? Are they good on game day? Do they do a good job of game planning and helping teach the assistants on your staff how to teach that game plan to the players? That's critical. It's not just calling plays in the game. It's doing that part of it.

And then we all have to coach a position. So you have to develop the players at your position fundamentally and technically. Not only just teaching them the game plan of what to do, but how do you need to do it. And then recruiting is such a big factor in what we all do. So, it's a lot more than just one particular thing of calling plays that make somebody a real asset on your staff.

Q. Coach, you alluded to this a little bit earlier. You've been through this 15-game season several times now. How do you prepare your players physically and mentally for the long season? When does that preparation begin?

SABAN: Well, we changed our approach last year in terms of starting to cut down practices a little bit earlier in the season, giving the players days off when we could before certain games.

We use a Catapult system here, and we sort of try to continue to evaluate where our players are relative to their explosive movements, making sure we don't get them too wore out.

So we've changed our approach a little bit from beginning to end. We probably condition a little less, trying to save our players throughout the year.

I don't know the formula exactly, but I know that if we can look at our Catapult system and make sure our players are not going down in terms of what they're able to do, then we're sort of at least maintaining what we need to maintain to be able to be competitive.

On the transition between offensive coordinators in the last year:

SABAN: I think that every week we are trying to put our guys in the best position that we possibly can to create the kind of balance offensively that makes us difficult to defend, and I think that our offensive staff has done a good job of that for the most part. But again, we are going to play some of the more challenging defensive teams that we will have to face down the road here. At this point, we have done a pretty good job offensively, but I think that it is important that everybody stays focused on improving and coming up with the kind of game plans and systems that are going to be effective against very good defensive teams.

On Alabama's young defense and No. 1 national rankings in defensive statistics:

SABAN: Well I don't look at this like you all look at it. Where we're ranked in defense doesn't really matter to me. I look at how we play, the mistakes that we make, the things that we need to get better on. I'm concerned about covering the people that we play the next game, playing well in the next game, because none of that stuff matter if you don't play well in the next game. So the challenge for us is the next game. That's what I'm focused on, that's what I'm looking at, that's what our entire staff is trying to do, and I think that needs to be the focus of our players. You start feeling good about where you are because you won the last tournament, but that doesn't mean you're going to win the next one. You start feeling entitled and you don't prepare the right way to do the right things then you don't play as well.

So our focus is on what we need to do to play well in this game. None of that other stuff matters. It only matters at the end—what was the whole body of work that you could do on a consistent basis, and none of the rest of it matters. We're going to play a lot better teams and a lot better offensive teams in the future and we're going to be challenged in different ways. I'm concerned about reacting to those challenges properly, not what we've done last week or the week before. So I'd appreciate it if we don't have to talk about that anymore, where we're ranked or what we're doing or what we did. I'm looking at what we're going to do.

On what goes on during the halftime of a game:

SABAN: Nobody's resting about anything. The first thing is that the coaches meet on adjustments that we need to make. That probably lasts three or four minutes. We probably meet six or eight minutes with the players in general, and go over every issue that we've had on both sides of the ball and on special teams. Then each individual coach takes his players probably for a couple of minutes, to specifically talk about things that they may have to adjust to, and then probably a minute or two prior to going out, I'll say what I have to say. That's pretty much what happens, and it's pretty much the same all the time.

On the few carries Richardson and Ingram had:

SABAN: When the game goes like the game went and you get behind 21-3, what is the priority? Is it to get those guys their carries or is to try to get back in the game? When you get behind 21-3 are you trying to get back in the game or are you trying to make sure Mark Ingram and Trent Richardson get their carries? What's the priority? To me it's to get back in the game. Sometimes the game determines that and sometimes, like last year when we had all the yards against South Carolina rushing, it's because we were ahead of the game and we were taking the air out of it because they couldn't stop us from running the ball so someone gained 200-plus yards. It was different circumstances in the game. We have a game plan to utilize all our players. We have lots of good players. We have three really good receivers, three really good runners, and I think we have to utilize all those things and take what the defense gives us.

If they're going to have the defense up there to stop us from running the ball and we need to throw the ball to beat them, then we have to do that. It's not about this guy's going to carry the ball this many times and that guy's going to carry the ball that many times. No matter what, that's hard to do and we want those guys to make a lot of plays. Whether they're catching the ball, whether they're running the ball, they have to do their share so that other players can be successful when it comes to their blocking and being a complete player at their position.

On looking back at preseason, were there any unknowns they came together during the season:

SABAN: I think you always sort of have questions and concerns about your team every year. There is always going to be some area of your team that you are trying to rebuild. It's always going to create opportunities for other players on your team and you never know for sure how that group is going to come together or how those young players are going to respond. The offense line was always sort of something that we talked about. Seldom did we have any kind of media gathering where somebody didn't ask about the concern they had about the quarterback position. There weren't always a lot of questions about the defense because there were a lot of guys coming back on the defense.

Now next year, I'm sure there will be a lot of questions about that because there's going to be lots of opportunities for other guys to play, relative to who leaves the team. I think you always have that in college. Your team is always changing and you really want to develop and you're always going to have those questions and you have those questions throughout the course of the year when you lose a significant player for a game, or for a season, or for several games. Just like we've had opportunities when we mentioned Peek missing games, Michael Williams did a really good job. Dont'a Hightower has missed 9 games and we had three or four guys that have sort of filled in various roles that he had, but they were question marks at the time.

I think you always have that on your team. It's sort of ever-evolving and ever-changing and I feel like we've been very fortunate this year that just about in every opportunity that was created somebody stepped up to the challenge and the other players on the team sort of helped them do the things they needed to do in order to be able to fulfill their role and responsibility to the team. But, you always have those questions.

On value of being an understudy for two years at quarterback and how Greg McElroy has handled that role:

SABAN: I think that any player improves, regardless of his role. Obviously, you never really want to play and player until he is ready to play. I think to have patience to develop at any position is probably something that most players don't like to have, but in a lot of cases probably need and some realize they need it and some don't. I think in Greg McElroy's case, because he is such an intelligent, fine young man, that he realizes what he has to do to improve, and he has improved in our system dramatically in the two years that we have been here, leading up to his opportunity.

I think some of them have enough foresight, even though sometimes we have that conversation about guys not understanding consequences of their behavior. You have freedom of choice, but don't have freedom of consequence. I have said that one before. He has enough foresight to realize, that even what he did two years ago, last year, every time he got an opportunity, every time he's gotten an opportunity in the spring, that he was eventually going to be the guy that goes out there and plays. I don't think there is any substitute for experience, and I don't think there is any substitute for the fact that as he gets experience and makes plays, he's going to become more confident and the players around him are going to become more confident in him. I think with that, his leadership will be more effective, and he will be a very effective player.

The Coaching Profession

Q. Just a follow-up on the coaching profession. You have a young man who's a graduate assistant and thinking of becoming a graduate assistant and wanted to be a head coach in college football. With the nature of the profession now, what would be your advice to him?

SABAN: I think the only advice I could give someone is try to do the things that I did when I started out as a graduate assistant and try to work hard and do the things that you need to do. Whatever your responsibility is, do them well so that people recognize the fact that you may be capable of developing into a good teacher and a good coach and a good recruiter. I guess that's the only advice I could give anyone.

It's a tough profession to break into, but I think guys have to be willing to sacrifice and get experience. I started out as a graduate assistant at Kent State. That was my first job at Kent State. I thought, when I got a job at Syracuse, that was a really big thing, and I've been really fortunate to get a lot of opportunities a lot of good places, but I've always tried to work hard and do a good job for the people I work for. I think that's the most important thing anyone can do.

Q. It seems like that's pretty much what happened with Coach McElwain, in which he accepted the job and still comes back and coaches in the Championship Game. Just kind of what it means to you to have him come back for that?

SABAN: It speaks volumes of his character and his professionalism. He did accept the job there -- we might not have even played in the SEC Championship Game that year. I can't even remember. You know, he got the job, and we did everything we could to help him get the job. He came back and did a fabulous job, and we won the National Championship.

Q. Jim was cutting up in here with us. What was he like in the coach's room? Was he as lighthearted as he is with us in the media?

SABAN: Jim is a really serious, attention-to-detail sort of guy that has a fantastic sense of humor. And I think that's always appreciated when you have coaches that are like that. It always creates a great balance on a staff when you have some guys that are serious, some guys that are maybe yell a little more and other guys are maybe a little quiet in the way they teach and some guys are funny and some guys are dry. It's the combination of all those things that I think makes a successful staff. You certainly don't want to have all everybody the same or everybody that wants to be like the head coach.

Everybody needs to be themselves, and I think having diversity in personalities on the staff is really healthy, and Jim was always a guy that had a great sense of humor and made other people feel really comfortable on our staff.

On the emphasis of finishing games in the fourth quarter:

SABAN: It's a part of the philosophy of the program since we've been here for five years. We want to win in the fourth quarter, that we have a fourth quarter program which is basically the strength and conditioning program that we do in the offseason, summertime. I think we try to get our players to believe that the hard work they do is going to contribute to their ability to be more physical for longer, and to finish games better, and that's something that we try to build as a part of the program. Each one of these things stands for something - commitment, discipline, toughness, pride, work. All of those things are really important to being able to win in the fourth quarter, and we are trying to sell our players on that.

On how other coaches tend to want to simplify things when they have a young defense:

SABAN: Last year we made a lot of mistakes, but I think that we grew from making those mistakes. I have confidence in the players, and I have confidence in the players' ability to learn. I think that a lot of coaches sometimes say that they're making it simple, but I never wanted to be a guy that was making it simple but then not putting the players in the best position to be successful. You don't want to make it so simple that they don't have a chance.

We have probably always erred on the other side, but I think that when you do, you are actually developing a greater capacity for them in terms of the amount of information that they can handle and what they understand and can adapt to in the game when things don't happen in the game exactly like you thought that they might. In the last two years, it has taken a lot of adaptability on defense because we end up seeing, especially at the beginning of the game a lot of different things than what we practiced for. The fans might not notice that. Now that resource of information the guys have to go back and draw on is better. If we had made it simple, they wouldn't know what to do, so the concepts that they have learned sometimes they can apply. It's very beneficial to them.

Saban on how he hires new assistant coaches.

SABAN: I think that knowledge and experience is really important. I think people look for that, but I also look for people that are going to be a good fit for us in terms of how they are going to fit with the other coaches on the staff, how they get along with people, what kind of relationships are they going to be able to build in the organization – players and coaches wise – to make people want to achieve at a high level. And I think the right people for us are the people that are willing to do it the Alabama way.

My sense of it is, what I see happening a lot, sometimes people want to do it the way they do it, the way they've had success with. We want people that will come here and do it the way we do it, the way our players are accustomed to do it, what they've bought in to and what they made commitment to. So unless we're looking for input to change something, we're bringing people to do what we do. That's a big part of the fit.

Saban on managing your time

SABAN: We've learned through the years you can't work all the time, which used to be a problem for me. We take advantage of the little time we have in the summer, and it's been very beneficial.

When I first started out as a head coach, I wanted to be successful and do a good job so badly that it was sort of all-in and nothing else. That wasn't good for anybody. It wasn't good for me. It wasn't good for our staff.

Through the years, I've had to learn, maybe the hard way sometimes. Balance is really healthy in anything that you do. I actually think it's now better for family, staff, staff's family and me personally. Hopefully, we can continue to do this for a while and stay healthy enough to do it, because we certainly do enjoy it.

Dealing With People

On the need for positive reinforcement:

SABAN: I just had a meeting yesterday with our team to reiterate to them how well I think they're doing this summer, working hard. Everybody's all into doing things the way we want to do them. Not a lot of negative energy around. A lot of positive energy, character and leadership. To continue to build relationships between players and players or players and coaches. Every player wants to know his coach knows how well he's doing. To communicate, to see it, to value it, to notice it and reinforce it is really something we all need to do more of. Catch them doing it right. That's something that's been pretty easy to do.

I think this will benefit our team in the future. It's important for players to do the right thing, the right time, the right way and do it all the time. To have a vision for what they want to accomplish and understand the fine process of things they have to do personally, academically and athletically. It takes a lot of discipline to be able to execute that every day, and that's something we try to get our players to buy into.

Discipline is a funny thing. It's not only doing the right thing, the right way, the right time all the time, it's making choices and decisions we all make every day. Discipline to me is, here's something I know I'm supposed to do that I really don't want to do, and can you make yourself do it? Over here, there's something you know you're not supposed to do that you want to do, can you keep yourself from doing it?

This is the decision-making that creates a moral compass for all of us to help us do the right things, to help us stay focused on the process of what we need to do to accomplish our goals. It's something that's certainly going to be important for our team to do a good job of if we're going to be able to have the kind of team we're going to have.

Saban on how he's changed when it comes to dealing with people:

SABAN: As a head coach, probably the biggest thing that I've changed in is just an overall understanding of human behavior and how people react the best. It's not always being overly intense or trying to intimidate people into doing better. Or it's more about helping them have a vision for what they want to accomplish and sell them on the process of what they need to do to accomplish it and having the discipline on a day-to-day basis to try to carry it out, which is more the approach that we use with players and coaches and people that we have to work with.

If everybody has a similar vision for what they want to accomplish, it's certainly easier to get everybody to buy into the process of things that they need to do to do it and their dedication and determination to stick with that on a day-to-day basis, which is really about discipline to execute.

Q. How do you feel like you've evolved, if that's the right word, as a head coach over the years, what are the important qualities you need in working with the staff, and in terms of just dealing with the university and the athletic department in general?

SABAN: I've been very fortunate, wherever I've been, that we've always had a great administration, whether it's great presidents, very good athletic directors, people who were really trying to serve and help us set the table for what we needed to do to be successful.

And we have a great team in Alabama, but I felt the same way when I was at LSU, Michigan State or wherever we've had opportunities in the past. And so that part of it really has not been difficult, because of the quality of people that we've been fortunate to work with.

I think as a head coach, probably the greatest thing that, or the biggest thing that you change or I've changed in is, just an overall understanding of human behavior and how people react the best. And it's not always being overly intense or trying to intimidate people into doing better or it's more about helping them sort of have a vision for what they want to accomplish and sell them on the process of what they need to do to accomplish it and sort of having the discipline on a day-to-day basis to try to carry it out, which is more the approach that we use with players and coaches and people that we have to work with.

And I think if everybody has a similar vision for what they want to accomplish, it's certainly easier to get everybody to buy into the process of things that they need to do to do it and their dedication and determination to stick with that on a day-to-day basis, which is really about discipline to execute.

On the importance to keeping Phillip Sims' attitude positive, given that he's a play away from starting:

SABAN: I think that's very important. I think every player needs to know, it's probably more difficult when you're not the starter, or you didn't start the game, to be prepared to play the game as it is for the guy that knows he's going to go out there and play. I think it takes a tremendous amount of maturity, takes a competitive personality that you're driven to want to be the best and will continue to work to be the best at your position, regardless of the circumstance you find yourself in, and that you can't be result-oriented and say that because I'm where I am now, that defines me. That doesn't define you. You define yourself in terms of who you want to be, what you want to be and how you want to go about doing it.

There was an interesting thing I saw on ESPN that Derek Jeter said, `If you want to be the best, good enough is just not good enough.' We don't want anyone out there just being good enough. We want you to be the best player you can be. That's the goal of the program. That should be the goal of the player, and that's what we want every player to do. It's just as hard for the backup right tackle to get ready to play the game knowing that that guy can go down too.

Pressure, Anxiety, & Emotion

Q. You and Urban are good at coaching in these big games. I'm sure that's an acquired skill. But can you talk about, I guess, when you got passed the anxiety in coaching in big pressure games like this, or do you still get butterflies before a big game like this?

SABAN: I get butterflies before every game. I get butterflies before every game that we play. I'm shaking my leg right now. And I would be shaking it on any Friday of any given game that we play, because to a coach, you feel like that game that you're playing that day is the biggest game that you have that particular year. It's the most important game because it's the game that you're playing now.

And your struggle as a coach is to always keep the people in your organization, including the players, the coaches and everybody else that works, not to think like regular people think; that it's time to take it easy this week because we play so and so.

You know, you're constantly trying to keep everybody playing to a standard of excellence to be the best that they can be so you can continue to improve as a team so that you will be in a better position when you do get in a game like this, if you can create that opportunity to play your best football. And that you've done it on a consistent basis and you have confidence in your ability to do that.

So I know that externally this game means a lot to a lot of people. And we never lose sight of that. But from our standpoint, how we get our team ready really can't change that much, because if there was a better way to do it, why wouldn't we do it the fifth week, or why didn't we do it against Ole Miss or LSU or whoever else we played. I think it would be an indictment on us if you discovered we didn't use the best techniques to win every one of those games.

Q. What in this time of preparation do you look for from your players to determine if-- to get clues as to whether their execution is going to be where you want it? Is it simply what they do in practice? Is it comments that you hear made? Is it an overall demeanor? And what has that been like?

SABAN: Well, I think it's where we need to be. And you never are quite sure at this stage where your team is. You can only speculate.

But I've liked the way we've prepared. I think we are where we need to be. We'll never know for sure until we get out there and start playing.

And it's not just what you do during the preparation but what you do during the game. Because every game is going to create some challenges and some opportunities to overcome adversity. And if you're a great competitor-- you can't be a great competitor if you can't overcome adversity.

And that kind of mindset is going to be very, very important, because every game I think we played against LSU in the last five comes right down to the wire, some kind of way. Whether we won, they won, it doesn't make any difference, there's one common theme: all the games come right down to the wire.

So you have to be prepared to sustain your performance for 60 minutes in the game, and I don't think that's all going to be just about emotion. A lot of that is about competitive character.

Q. What has been the final main message that you've given your players going into this game?

SABAN: Well, I think that what we're trying to get our players to do is stay focused on the things that are going to help them play well in the game and not be affected by external factors, all the things that are going on around this game, and it's a big game, there's no doubt, for every player that's created an opportunity to play in it on both sides. But you've got to focus on the next play and do what you have to do to do your job to help your team be successful.

I think that's where you want the players to stay focused, and that's the message that we're trying to give them so that they can go out and have the best opportunity to be successful.

On how much of the turnover battle is mental:

SABAN: I think it's a consciousness and awareness as much as anything. I think it gets a little bit contagious and sometimes that becomes physiological. When you start getting a lot of turnovers everybody is focused on that and you continue to be able to create plays, and get them and I think sometimes when you don't get them, and you talk about all the time that we are not getting them, that kind of gets to be a roadblock in your mind about being able to get them. So I think your mindset has a lot to do with it, your confidence and your ability to do it and have an experience of doing it are all things that can contribute to it in a positive way. I think it's the same thing when you're a runner, if you get the reputation of being a fumbler - sometimes that's hard to shake. How much is that physical, how much is psychological, I'm not sure, but sometimes if you tell somebody that they are something for long enough they start believing it. So I think sometimes you have to be careful about trying to be technical and how you correct people rather than branding them in any kind of way.

On slow starts on the road:

SABAN: I think it's important to start fast in any game that you play. I think it's also important to finish strong, because I think every play in the game is important. You certainly want to be able to get off to a good start wherever you play, whenever you play. I don't really know exactly what the reason might be for slow starts. I think I know. I think that you need to have some calm in the midst of chaos sometimes when you play on the road because there are a lot of other distractions, and I think mature players that have experience probably handle that a little bit better. Now that we've played on the road a few times, I thought we handled it a little bit better at Tennessee. Hopefully we'll handle it a little bit better this time. It's all about your ability to focus on the task at hand and not be distracted by all the things that are going on around you. There are a lot of difficult places to play in this league, and it takes a lot of maturity to be able to stay focused and do those things. Hopefully our team will continue to mature and be able to play better and better as we play on the road. I think it's going to be critical in this game for sure.

On avoiding clutter in your own mind:

SABAN: I really don't think about stuff like that, actually. When you work as many hours as we do and there are as many things that are going on, whether it is recruiting, or getting ready for practice or like I said the other day forgetting your anniversary, there is a lot going on. We work a lot of time and we have a lot of people who make a lot of contributions, our coaching staff and everybody else, in management and scheduling and what you're doing. I try to pride myself in the ability to focus on the next event and try to do that as well as we can so that everybody in the organization will have a chance to do as well too. I think anticipation of issues and problems is really important in trying to do that, so you are always trying to think one step ahead and be well organized when it comes, so you're getting the most out of the work that you're doing, whether it's with the staff, or with the players, or with recruiting or any of that stuff. I don't have a lot of time to think about that. I really try not to think about it and I really don't think about it.

Anticipation is what's coming up next. We have a practice tomorrow. What are we going to work on in practice? What's going to be the focus? There are a lot of things you need to cover and that's the type of stuff I'm thinking about on a day-to-day basis. We are going to evaluate practice today and decide what we can do to help make it a better practice, as well as individually, how we can make some of these corrections that would help someone play better. Also, reinforce the positive plays, so the guys can feel good about what they did accomplish in a good way. So, that's not ever been one of my issues. It's always been the next thing, the next challenge, the next issue and the next play.

I honestly believe that if I'm blessed with anything, it's the ability not to get complacent and not to get sort of comfortable because of the perfectionist that I feel like I am in terms of how we operate and what we do. That's not easy sometimes when you've got that kind of personality, but it is what it is, I guess is what I usually say.

Practice

On quarterbacks getting equal reps:

SABAN: I really think one of them has to come out there first, but I don't think that necessarily means that guy is the starter. I think both guys will play in the game and we will have a plan for both guys to play in the game. I think it's out of fairness to them that they both get an opportunity to play in this game, it's kind of what we've talked about. I don't think one guy has clearly separated himself from the other and I think that both guys will be given the chance to play in the game, but they will know exactly how they are going to play in the game and the consequences of their play will not be a factor as to whether they continue to play in whatever is programmed for them to play. In other words, I don't want any player out there looking over his shoulder thinking, `If I make one bad play, you are going to pull me out of the game.' We're going to let the guys play, and they're going to play their role. Then we'll assess where we think they are, and if there was some way one guy responded better than another that makes a difference then we'll evaluate that. That's what is going to happen. And I hate that it's going to happen, but in fairness to the players, I think both deserve an opportunity.

On quarterback preparation and live hitting:

SABAN: Well you know I look out on the practice field lots of days and I say, `Well would that guy have made that decision if he was going to get splattered on that play?' There are some disadvantages to putting a black shirt on a quarterback and not allowing him to get hit. At the same time, quarterback is an important position, and do you want to risk making them live to create an issue? Because quarterback is a bit of a defenseless position too, because you aren't in a position like everyone else. You could play nose guard, but you're in position to defend yourself every play. So is the right corner, and the tight end, and every receiver, but the quarterback really isn't. To make him live, and because someone else didn't block the right guy, he's going to get blasted and have an opportunity to break a hand or a finger or something that's going to put him out. I never thought that that risk/reward was all that worth it. The down side of that is that they haven't gotten hit that much. Ball security is something you have to coach in those circumstances and situations. They're going to get hit now in the game, and I just don't really know the best way to do that because I would like for them to get hit, but I would like for them to not get hurt.

On Will Lowery going from scout team to an on-field contributor:

SABAN: Will has done a really good job of - I think there are some guys on your team that just have the capabilities of being responsible to do a job. They love to play, they play hard but they play smart, they do the right things and they try to do it the way they're coached to do it. I think in putting all those things together you come up with a pretty efficient player that does his job on a pretty consistent basis, and that's what Will has done. We knew that he had the chance to be a guy athletically that could contribute. I think the circumstance in the secondary with so many guys leaving last year and so many new guys coming in sort of put him in a position where he could get a lot of repetitions and he certainly took advantage of his opportunity and had done a really good job for us to this point.

On his biggest question with the team that fall camp didn't answer:

SABAN: What the maturity is? What the identity is going to be? The things that I have talked about before. What is the chemistry of the team? Are the young players going to mature? Are there enough older players that have played to provide the leadership and example to affect those guys and help their maturity? I think those are the big things. We have some guys that are in critical spots as specialist that it will be interesting to see how they grow and develop in their confidence and what they do to be performers for us.

On how much more he learns about the team in the game day setting:

SABAN: I think that is ultimately what you have to learn about them. How are they going to compete on game day? I've said this before, some guys play better when the game comes, and some guys who practice pretty well don't compete nearly as well when the game comes and I don't think you can figure that out until the game comes. If hot peppers give you a belly ache, you can't figure it out until you eat hot peppers.

On role of scout team:

SABAN: I don't think you can get ready to play and prepare for a game if you don't get a great look by your look squad. It's a pretty thankless job, too. Most of those guys don't get to play in the game. They don't win awards. They don't get their names in the paper, although we try to create awards and try to have scout team players of the week on offense, defense and special teams every week, so that those guys do get some positive self-gratification for what they do for the team. They can be on the war daddy board if they do a good job in practice all week and are recognized by the coaches and their teammates for that. We can't get ready for the game if we don't get a good look from our look squads. I think probably those guys don't get enough accolades. They don't get enough attention from any of us, including the coaches, who spend our time coaching the guys who are going to play in the game and those guys do a fantastic job. And probably the most difficult task that anybody has is probably those guys in terms of the perseverance they have to have relative to what they get out of it.

On entertaining the thought of actually scrimmaging with a five-week layoff before a bowl game:

SABAN: I think that we have discussed that quite a bit. That's not something that I have done in prior years and certainly at this point you would not want to scrimmage and lose players because you're creating a game-like situation which could create that. What we have discussed is trying to create as game-like a situation as we can in the spirit of safety for our players and having one situation probably the last practice before we go home, that simulates a lot of the situations and game-like stuff. Now whether we tackle people to the ground and do things like it's a real scrimmage - I think the greatest opportunities to get injured is when people are on the ground. We want to try and avoid that, but we also feel like we need to do something that's very game-like that's going to help our players take the next step of getting ready for this game.

Maximizing Talent

Q. There's a lot of fascination between the contrast of the two teams' styles. You guys are seen as kind of a throwback; Florida throws it around, runs, passes. Do you appreciate that, or is there too much being made of that?

SABAN: I really think that it's not so much the approach, because we've had teams before that threw it all around, too, and when we were in this game in 2001 we couldn't get a pass off, but we had four great wide-outs. I think three or four of them were first or second ground drafts picks, and we had a good quarterback and we won the SEC Championship based on that, and we weren't a very good defensive team. But we threw the ball for a lot of yards and a lot of gains and made a lot of big plays. But that's what that teams could do.

I think the teams you're talking about now, the contrast in style is because both teams know who they are and they play to the style that they need to have success. Sometimes you can recruit to a style, but you never put your style ahead of the personnel, because it's all about the players. What we do allows us to be the most successful, and I think what Florida does with their players allows them to be most successful.

They have a unique guy playing quarterback to do what they do. You can think they don't run the ball, but you'd better be able to stop them running, because if you want to talk about throwback offense, they're running the single wing. Last time I was involved in a single wing I was ten years old playing pee-wee ball, and I was the quarterback. So I understand that offense a little bit from back then, and my dad was the coach. I don't know who's got a throwback offense. Now, they do empty it out and spread it out and we didn't do all that back then, and it's a lot more difficult to defend when they're spread out, but their quarterback, who's a good passer as well as a good runner, really allows them to play a style that would be difficult to match unless you have the right kind of personnel to do it.

I think the compliment here is that both teams play with a style that allows them to be most successful.

On how the team is able to continually come out to great starts:

SABAN: At times, we have started really well in games and at other times we have started three-and-out on offense in the Michigan game for example. We then came back and played extremely well. Defensively last year, the first series of the game was usually the worst for us. This year we have gotten off to a pretty good start defensively. I don't know if there is any rhyme or reason for it. We definitely try to prepare our players for what they're expected to see.

I think that one of the things that contributed to it was that we always saw something different that we hadn't practiced against. This year we haven't seen as much of that kind of stuff so I think the players are a little comfortable starting the game relative to what they've practiced and that may have something to do with it.

On not trailing in games up to that point in the season:

SABAN: I think that we are constantly trying to teach our players that you play the next play, you are worried about the scoreboard, you are not worried about the circumstance in the game - that is an external factor - you need to focus on what you need to do to execute the very next play - whether you're ahead in the game or behind in the game, that really doesn't matter.

That is something that we're constantly trying to instill in our players, from a competitive standpoint. If they have never been in a situation, I guess you don't know for sure how they are going to respond. I think it's about poise and confidence and just continuing to play in the game and having confidence that if you continue to do the right things and execute and pay attention to detail, and play together as a team you are going to have a chance to come back and be able to do the things you need to do to be successful.

On the key to getting out and starting fast in all three games so far:

What was the score after the first quarter last game? We didn't get off very fast. I remember it being 7-0 for a long time. Worried about whether we fumbled the punt or not so that they were going to get the ball in good field position and tie it up - with all those people dressed in red up there, screaming down our neck. I must have been at a different game. Was I at a different game or were we at the same game? I thought that it was a very tough game for the first quarter of the game.

I think that part of the way we play is that we want to try to wear people down as we go - psychologically as well as physically - in terms of our ability to execute, the kind of effort that we play with, the kind of toughness that we play with, the way we can sustain and persevere through a game and I think that's important. It is all part of the whole fourth quarter program, conditioning and strength and all the things that we work on so that we can have a team that can do those types of things. I have been happy with the way we have been able to do that in a couple of games - I didn't think in the second game we played particularly well in any aspect, not even in the second half. We want to continue to improve on those things.

3
OTHER COACHES & PLAYERS

Q. Talk about your relationship with Dabo, what he means to you, just watching him grow as a coach and as a player.

SABAN: Well, I have a lot of respect for Dabo, and I really got to know him really well in the last few years. When we first came to Alabama and he was an assistant coach at Clemson, he was a guy that I was very interested in hiring because of his reputation as a coach, as a person, as a recruiter, and he made a good decision to stay at Clemson because he eventually became the head coach.

But I also was interested in him because he was a former player at Alabama, and I always think it's good to have some of those people who connect you to different eras to be a part of your staff. But in the last few years, because we both have a place down at Boca and sometimes we have the same time off and we're able to get together family-wise and take a boat ride and talk about some of the issues and problems that we both sort of have to deal with, I have a tremendous amount of respect for him. I think he's done a fantastic job at Clemson in terms of how they develop players, the quality of players that they're able to recruit, and the good job that he does helping his players be successful, as well.

I really have as much respect for Dabo as anybody in our profession.

Q. Nick, this is in all likelihood the last time you and Kirby Smart will be on the same sideline. How will you look back on your relationship with him and how appropriate would it be to close out a championship?

SABAN: Well, Kirby has been with me a long time, all the way back to LSU days, Miami days, and the entire time we've been at Alabama, nine years. Kirby has done a fantastic job in every way in terms of relationships with players, developing players, recruiting players, doing a good job of implementing scheme, system, getting people to buy in and believe in. Kirby has done a fantastic job, and I certainly appreciate the fact that he's stuck here with us and done a really good job so far in trying to finish this year for our players, and I think that's the number one reason that he's here. I'm sure he's going to be a very, very successful head coach.

But these things are inevitable when you have really good assistant coaches that they work hard to aspire to have the next opportunity. I appreciate and respect the great job that they did for us, but it also makes you pleased and happy and proud to see them get an opportunity to do the things that they wanted to do.

You know, it's sort of like you have a son and he's moving away, and you want to see him do really, really well because we all go through stations of life where things change, so now someone else will have a better -- an opportunity. Kirby will have an opportunity. Somebody will have an opportunity to do what he does, and hopefully we can provide a little leadership and guidance that will help him along the way have a chance to be successful.

Q. Talk about your counterpart Mack Brown.

SABAN: Well, I think Mack, we have a tremendous amount of

respect for all that Mack has done in his career as a coach. Each place that he's been he has had a tremendous amount of success with a lot of consistency, and I think that he's very well-organized, runs a good program, is an outstanding recruiter and surrounds himself with very good people. And I think the consistency in performance that he's been able to accomplish at Texas and other places sort of, you know, proves that to -- that he has done a marvelous job of affecting people and getting them to give their best efforts to be successful.

Q. Do your former assistants, Will Muschamp, Derek Dooley, seek your advice about certain aspects of the job, even though they're now coaching your competition?

SABAN: I have a tremendous amount of respect for all the coaches that have worked for me and done a fantastic job, and am very happy to see them have opportunities because that's what they worked so hard for. That's what they did a great job for us.

We would not have had the success that we've had if it wasn't for the staff and coaches that worked for us in the past. So I have a tremendous respect and admiration for what those guys have done for me.

So when they do call or they do ask or we discuss things that may affect the future of college football, I'm always willing to be as helpful as I possibly can to helping them enhance their programs.

Look, I'm for everybody having a good program. And the idea that you have to dislike somebody to compete against them is not something I've ever really bought into. I like Derek Dooley, I like Will Muschamp, I like Jimbo Fisher, I like Mark Dantonio, I like Jayson Garrett. All these guys have worked for me somewhere along the line, and I would like to help them every way I could, have the best program they can have for their players. That's what college football is really all about.

It's our job to go create a good product of our own. Whether it's right or wrong, my dad said, You should always try to win the game based on your execution, not hope that the other guy's lack of execution is going to help you win the game, all right? So that's the way we've always kind of approached it.

So what they do, if we do what we're supposed to do, we'll still be sort of at the top of our game. So that's what we try to emphasize. We really do appreciate the contribution that those guys have made through the years to our success.

Q. I know your relationship with the Stoops family goes way back to the early'80s. Can you sort of talk about what you remember about Ron Stoops?

SABAN: Ron was a really good friend, defensive coordinator at Cardinal Mooney, and his uncle Bob, you know, I call him, which is Bob's uncle, was the head coach at South High School in Youngstown, and that was my recruiting area for many, many years.

And Ron was just a fantastic person and a really good coach and very well respected by all the players that he coached. And Bob was a good friend. And he's a little different than Ron in that he was a little bit of a free spirit.

So I remember that when I would be recruiting there, most of the time when the schools close you have to wait until people get home from work before you can go do home visits at night. I was an assistant at this time. So I used to meet Bob at the boiler room at South High School and used to play cards, gin rummy, until I could go on a home visit.

That was the kind of relationship I've had with them. When all these guys played at Iowa, the whole family-- I'm coaching at Michigan State as a defensive coordinator, the whole family would come to Michigan State and they'd all come to the house after the game.

So this is a relationship that goes way back for many, many years, and I think it's because of the respect that I had for the family and the quality of people that they were. And certainly have the same respect for the coaching fraternity that comes from that family, and obviously starts with Bob.

Q. Do you enjoy coaching against really close friends or is that more stressful mentally on you?

SABAN: To me, I value the relationships I have with other people probably more than anything else, especially at this station in my life. I think when you get a little older, you realize how important those relationships are.

I certainly value my relationship, whether it's Will Muschamp when we played against him or any other coach that's coached for me or that is a good friend of mine, like Gary Pinkel.

At the same time I never, ever have taken any of these games that we play personally. It's not personal. I respect them as a competitor. I hope they respect me as a competitor. I think they know when we play the game that we're both going to do the best we can to compete with our group the best that we can.

But that's part of what we respect about each other. When the game's over, that friendship is not affected by what happens in the game. At least it isn't for me. But maybe the respect grows in terms of the other person and the quality of work that they did.

So in one way I certainly respect the relationships, but in the other way I want to protect those relationships and never make the game personal with the people I'm coaching against.

Q. What's your reaction to Jim Harbaugh being hired at Michigan? We're getting a lot of questions, at least we are e-mail-wise, how much is a college football coach really worth

having a salary maybe up to $8million a year, we'll see what happens, what's your reaction to that and explain--

SABAN: First of all, I have a tremendous amount of respect for the Harbaugh family. I knew his dad when he was a secondary coach at Michigan and I was a secondary coach and we used to spend time together.

So to see both of the Harbaughs do really, really well as NFL coaches in Baltimore and San Francisco, tremendous amount of respect for the entire family, and Tom Crean, who is the head basketball coach in Indiana, is married to another Harbaugh coach, which I'm sure she does a good job of supporting him just like my wife does me.

And they were at Michigan State when we were there. He was an assistant for Tom Izzo, and we we're really good friends. So I've had a good relationship with the entire Harbaugh family for probably 30 years. So I'm happy and excited that someone of Jim Harbaugh's character and quality is going to come back and be a part of college football.

And I'm sure he'll do a fantastic job at the University of Michigan, which has great tradition. And I know he'll do a really good job there. From the college football coach standpoint and the financial question that you asked me, the only thing that I can say to that is, what kind of value do you create for the university? If you create value for the university and you look at it from that standpoint, then I think that there's a relative amount that someone's worth based on that.

And I don't really spend a lot of time trying to figure that out. So I really can't tell you exactly what that is or what it should be. But I think administrators probably have a better feel for that and have to make a determination as to what someone's worth relative to the value they create for their institution.

Q. Coach, wanted to first just get your reaction. I know you were asked about Les Miles last week on the SEC teleconference, but just your reaction to today's news about Mark Richt getting fired after a 9-3 season.

SABAN: Well, I don't know what the world is coming to in our profession. Mark Richt has been a really good coach and a really positive person in our profession for a long, long time. I think, when you win nine games, that's a pretty good season, especially with the body of work that he's been able to put together there for however many years he's been there, I think it's 15 or so.

I hate to see people that have the character and quality and ability to affect young people in a positive way like Mark Richt not be a part of our profession. People don't realize the importance of some of the other things that go into college coaching, whether it's helping develop young men as people, helping them develop careers off the field by graduating from school.

We all get it. We know we have to win games. Winning nine games is not bad, and he certainly won a lot of games for a long time. I hate to see these kinds of things.

On characteristics of a Mark Richt team:

SABAN: They are always very well coached. You are not going to find them out of position very much. They are sound and solid in everything they do. They are always physical. They always play with great effort and toughness. They are always going to have great skill players. That has always been a trademark of his teams. They have good quarterback play and great skill players of offense, a lot of players on defense who play with toughness and can run. They are well coached, discipline and are always going to be in the right spot. You are going to have to beat them and they are not going to beat themselves very much.

Q. Nick, I know you're not a big fan of questions that look back at things that happened 20 years ago. But do you remember at all what put Mark on your radar leading up to when you hired him as an assistant or what are some of the memories you have of his development as a coach while working on that stuff?

SABAN: I remember Mark when he played at Zanesville High School. I was the coach that recruited that area and he went to South Carolina. I think sometimes when you meet people, like I've known Bobby's family ever since I was 25 years old, recruiting Youngstown. His dad was a great defensive coordinator at Cardinal Mooney and Uncle Bob who was a coach at South High School.

So when you kind of know these people and you develop relationships with them, you never forget them. Mark coached at Kansas with Glen Mason who I coached with at Ohio State and done a really good job. I thought we were fortunate to be able to hire him and he did a fantastic job for us in the five years that we were there.

I always thought he'd do great if he ever got an opportunity to be a head coach. He's certainly done a lot better job at Michigan State than I ever could do. So he's done really well. I'm proud of him.

On his relationship with Gary Pinkel:

SABAN: Gary was actually one year behind me in school, so I was a senior when he was a junior. I have always had a tremendous amount of respect for the kind of person that Gary is. He was a hard worker and very smart football-wise. We spent one year as GAs and part-time coaches. We were not assistants, so I did have an opportunity to work with him, and I do think that Don James had a tremendous impact. I can't speak for Gary, but on me, in terms of my whole philosophy in dealing with players, personal development programs, academic support programs, talking about things relative to football as well as program oriented things, how to recruit, how to evaluate players. I learned a lot. When I first started coaching, Don

James was so well-organized that I just assumed that any place that you went, that's how everybody did things. When I left Kent State and went to other places, I was like, 'Wow, Coach James was way ahead of all of this.' I know Gary was exposed to the same thing and was with Coach James a lot longer, and I felt bad about leaving Toledo after one year and I knew the best person out there for that program would be Gary. I was just happy that he got the job, and he did fabulous job there for a long time and he has done a fabulous job at Missouri.

On Georgia State head coach Bill Curry:

SABAN: I think Bill Curry is a fantastic person. He's always, I think, been a class guy in everything that I've ever had any dealings with him, and he's always been very fair and honest with me. I've always had a tremendous amount of respect for him. When he was in broadcasting I got to visit with him on a few occasions, but I always felt like he did a great job when he was a coach. I always thought he was an outstanding, classy person with great character and has done a good job in everything that he's sort of tried to do. That's my impression of him.

On LSU defensive coordinator John Chavis:

SABAN: He's done a really good job there. They've always had good defensive teams, good defensive players. Bo Peleni did a really good job there for several years. He has a lot of experience, he's got a good system, he's very multiple and I think even this year being the second year that he's there the players probably feel a lot more comfortable with the system and execute it very well. He does a fantastic job. I've always had a tremendous amount of respect for him all the years he was at Tennessee and the great job that he did there. He has good players, but they all play pretty well and they're sound in what they do.

On his relationship with Michigan State head coach Mark Dantonio, who suffered a heart attack on Saturday:

SABAN: First of all, I haven't talked to him. I've tried to get in touch with him but it's been a little difficult, but our thoughts and prayers are with him and his family. He did a fantastic job for us a long time - five years at Michigan State and has been a very good coach everywhere he has been. He's done a great job at Michigan State and had a great win against Notre Dame. The one thing that I remember is he was always in a hell of a lot better shape than I was so that's kind of a wake-up call to me to make sure I'm doing the right things and taking care of myself. It was really kind of a shock because he was so into physical fitness, good health, and good conditioning all the time. Hopefully this will resolve and in a few weeks he'll be back to normal and won't have any future issues.

On appearing on Duke basketball head coach Mike Krzyzewski's radio show over the summer and what he admires in Coach K:

SABAN: I'm actually reading his book. I think he's another one of those iconic coaches, relative to what he does, whether it's John Wooden and people like that that you try to learn from. But anybody who has had as much success as he's had, relative to a full body of work over a long time, you're always interested and anxious to learn how they feel, learn how they see things and learn how they do things, whether it's philosophically or systematically. You learn something to implement and make your program better. I enjoyed that radio show, learned a lot, and I'm enjoying reading his book. It's a good book.

On his connections with offensive line coach Joe Pendry:

SABAN: Well Joe Manchin, who is the governor of West Virginia, was from my hometown and we grew up together, even though he was a few years older than me. Joe Pendry and Joe Manchin were roommates at West Virginia, both on football scholarship, when I was probably in eighth or ninth grade, so there is probably four or five years difference in age. So Joe used to come home with Joe Manchin, the governor, when I was in the ninth grade. I used to go see Joe play in freshman games because we had freshman games, that's Joe Manchin, and Joe Pendry was his roommate. So, I've known Joe from that time. I've known Sandi Pendry from that time. He's visited us at the lake and stayed at our house. We coached together at West Virginia for a while and now we have the opportunity to coach together here.

On if Pendry approached you about this job or did you approach him:

SABAN: Well, often times you have relationships with others in coaching and you call and ask about people and talk about people. I am not sure exactly how it came up, but I was talking to him about some other coaches and some other people and it just came up that he'd be interested in coming back and just wanted to be the offensive line coach. He's done a phenomenal job for us here.

On why Joe Pendry is a good coach:

SABAN: I think there are a lot of things, probably. He's a good teacher. He has a lot of experience. He's been around a lot of other good coaches and he'd probably be the first one to tell you that most of us learn what we know from someone else, which is knowledge and experience and being around good people, have good teaching progressions and teach in a way where the players can understand it and have the interest of the players at heart so they can get better. That's the one thing you can say about our offensive linemen here, they've all made a significant amount of improvement and played significantly well for us.

On Monte Kiffin's defensive philosophy:

SABAN: Well he actually gained fortune and fame as a very good defensive coordinator in college for many, many years and probably made some innovations in the game, relative to coordinating fronts and coverages and doing some things that nobody had done before. I remember going to visit him when he was at Arkansas and this was in the 1970s. In pro football, he sort of developed what's called Tampa Two, a coverage and way to play that was effective for a long time. Right now at Tennessee, they probably do a combination of both of those things. He's just a really good teacher, a really good coach and has a lot of knowledge and experience and has done a really good job this year helping their defense develop.

On his relationship with Steve Spurrier:

SABAN: I've known Steve for a long time. I was his assistant in the East-West game years ago. The year I went to LSU. Butch Davis and I were his two assistants. I've known Steve for a long time. I know his wife as well and so does Terry and we have a good relationship with them. He actually rode back on the LSU plane with me when we came back from the East-West game and they about blew the Gator plane up in Baton Rouge when it waiting there to pick him up and take him home. I have a lot of respect for him. He has done a great job every place he has been. We played against him at LSU when he was still at Florida. I think he is an outstanding coach and has done a really job at South Carolina.

On defensive coordinator Kirby Smart:

SABAN: First of all, guys that have been on my staff at three different places have gone way overboard, in terms of their loyalty in wanting to stay, because I am supposed to be really hard to work for. Just on that, I am really thankful that Kirby sticks around. Kirby has done a really good job. We hired Kirby at LSU when he had just coached maybe a year or something at Valdosta State and was a G.A. at Florida State. He has done a really good job. He's a hard worker. He certainly understands our system and can apply it in the game, which I think is the part of it that a lot of people really overlook. You can know a system and you can understand it and you can teach it, but there is a whole other level to be able to go into a game and apply it where it's effective. He's been around and he's done a really good job at that and I think it shows by how we play on the field.

On Les Miles getting fired:

SABAN: First of all, Les Miles is one of the most respected colleagues in terms of the rivalry we've had, the competition we've had, the great teams they've had. I kind of hated that the man wins a national championship, wins two SEC titles and doesn't make it through the season. It is what it is. I have a tremendous amount of respect for Les Miles, what he was able to accomplish there, the number of wins.

This is very similar to Georgia firing Mark Richt when he averages 10 wins a season. I guess this is the time we live in. Everybody needs to know that. It doesn't minimize to any degree the amount of respect we have for the job Les Miles did at LSU and the great competitive teams he's had for a long time, the amount of success he's had. I certainly wish him and his family well.

That's not really for me to say one way or the other. We feel fortunate to have the kind of team we have at Alabama that's created an atmosphere and environment where our players have a chance to be successful personally, athletically and academically. I think we've created a lot of value for our players. Because of that, we've had some really good players. Those guys have competed well and played well. We've had some great coaches.

Because of the team we have, from our administration to the players and coaches, all those things contribute. It's not just about who the head coach is. That's why we've been successful. It's a challenge for us to try to be successful. I can't really comment on anybody else's standard on what they want to accomplish or what they want to do.

Q. How has Kirby Smart evolved in your years together on staff as a coach?

SABAN: Well, Kirby's been with me for a long, long time. So I've been getting a lot of these memory-jogging questions this week, which I guess there's a name for that when you get older, but I won't elaborate.

But you know, Kirby was really enthusiastic, bright, good teacher, related well with players when he first started. And because he's bright, he really not only learned the system, but he also understood how to implement it and really understands football very, very well. Understands offensive football very, very well, because I think being a defensive coach, I think that's what you have to do.

His leadership with what he's responsible for, which is the defense, for us has been outstanding. Got good relationships with the players. They respond well to him. He's sound in how he goes about the things that we do and we've worked together for a long, long time. He's as good an assistant coach and as loyal an assistant coach as I've ever had on my staff.

You want to ask something else?

Q. It sounds like -- talking about your relationship --

SABAN: I think any time -- people that work together on a staff, it's for a long time, it's like part of your family. I talked about this at the lunch on. Nobody's ever looked at it this way, but we're kind of bigamists as coaches. We're married, we have families, but we're also married to our job. And you have to be married to your job and spend a lot of time with the relationships of the players and the coaches and the people.

So if you can just sort of look at it that way, you have a family there, too, so you do develop relationships and you do care about these people, and you care about their families and you care about their well-being. You understand their goals and aspirations and like to help give them direction so that they have a chance to reach those goals and aspirations.

So I'm always happy to see anyone on our staff who has done a great job for us get the opportunity that they have worked so hard for.

Urban Meyer

Q. Obviously, you have ties to Bill Belichick. Urban Meyer has also befriended him. Do you see any Belichick tendencies in Coach Meyer? What do you think he's been able to do to kind of turn Florida into the national championship program it's become?

SABAN: I think, first of all, Urban is a great coach, surrounds himself with outstanding people, has a good staff. They work about as hard as anybody I know. I mean, we're kind of a blue-collar program. We have a tremendous amount of respect for that.

I know that Bill is like that. But I think Urban was like that before he ever met Bill. I think that's why they have a tremendous amount of success in recruiting, and they do a phenomenal job of developing the players that they have.

So I can't make any comparisons to know what their relationship is. I don't know that. I know I coached for four years with Bill Belichick. He was an outstanding coach. I probably learned as much from him in terms of organization, football, management, defining roles so that people understand what's expected of them, as anybody that I've ever been around. Certainly, you know, his success proves that what he does, the process that he uses, it's very effective.

Q. I was wondering, obviously when Urban was at Florida, you guys were always going after the best players in recruiting. And we had a kid specifically from the Chattanooga area, Vonn Bell, that you guys were interested in. And he wound up going to Ohio State. I was just kind of seeing if you still go up against him a lot in recruiting and what you remember about Vonn Bell?

SABAN: Well, we thought Vonn Bell was an outstanding player and certainly wanted him in our program. I think if he was in our program right now he would be a very productive player for us.

We see Urban a lot in recruiting. And I know last year there were two or three players that we wanted that they got. And there was a couple that they wanted that we got.

And I think that if you have one of the top programs and I've always had a tremendous amount of respect for the energy in recruiting that Urban and his staff and their organization has in trying to go after some of the best players, identifying them and going after them.

Obviously they've done a great job of recruiting there and that's why they have a very good team and that's why they're going to be in this playoff.

So we have a tremendous amount of respect for the way they recruit.

Q. Last time you guys faced each other in a championship setting, the 2009 SEC Championship Game that sort of elevated your program to the national title level. What did that mean for your program to mean that game and then to go on and win that first national title?

SABAN: I think Florida was a dominant program at the time. We lost the SEC Championship Game in 2008, so this was sort of a rematch. They went on to win the National Championship.

I think maybe the two best teams might have been playing in the SEC Championship Game in 2009. We played a phenomenal game. Our players did a fantastic job. Our coaches did a fantastic job in that game. They went on to win the National Championship.

I think the combination of-- look, I put a tremendous amount of value on winning the SEC. I think it was a great accomplishment for our team this year to win the SEC. It's a special league. There was a lot of good teams, and our players and our team overcame a lot to do it, and it was no different in that year. I think we were ranked one and two, if I'm remembering correctly in both those championship games.

So it was a playoff game in a sense and they won one and we won one. Both teams went on to win a championship.

Q. What can you take from your previous matchups with Urban if anything?

SABAN: Well, I think that obviously they have a very good team, very good players. They're very well coached, which is nothing different from any other team that we've faced that Urban has coached, because he does a fantastic job with his players and coaches to put an outstanding product on the field.

There are some similarities with what they do, especially offensively in terms of what they did when they were at the University of Florida, what he did.

But they have different players. They do a great job of utilizing the talent and the players that they have. So on special teams and offense, there are some similarities. Probably not as much on defense. But we're playing against this team now. So we've tried to prepare based on what we need to do to play well against the players that they have and the system that they use right now, which is very effective and they've been very productive offensively, play very good defense, and I think very explosive and make a lot of plays on special teams, which is very typical of Urban Meyer-coached teams.

Q. Between yourself and Coach Meyer the two have won six national titles over your career, how would you describe the relationship the two of you have built over the years?

SABAN: I didn't really know Urban all that well when he was at Florida. Mostly because I'm sure you've heard this story before, but when I was coaching at the Houston Oilers in '88,'89, whenever that was, and took the head coaching job at the University of Toledo, after the'89 season, my wife, Terry, who has always been very involved in what we do, and I was finishing the season with the Oilers, I wasn't paying a whole bunch of attention of what I was going to do when I was going to Toledo, trying to do a good job for the players we had. We had a playoff team. And Urban called.

He was a graduate assistant somewhere. And Terry talked to him, and I came home one night after preparation for one of our games at the Oilers, and she said, You know, I talked to a really interesting guy today, Urban Meyer, and I really do think you should talk to him when you hire your staff at Toledo.

And I was so kind of caught up and busy in what I was doing I never really followed up on that. And obviously that was a huge mistake on my part, because he's a fantastic coach and he's done a really, really good job. But we did have the opportunity to work one of the national championship games, I think it was the Auburn/Oregon game when Cam Newton was playing at Auburn, I guess that was 2010.

So we spent three or four days together and really got to know him and his wife and really saw what a really good person he is and he's got a lot of really good qualities in terms of being a successful person at what he does and developed a tremendous amount of respect for him not just as a coach but as the kind of person that he is and a great work ethic that he has and how well organized he is in terms of his program.

So it was no surprise to me that he got back into coaching a very good situation at Ohio State that has a great tradition and that it would not take him long to establish one of the top programs in the country, which he's certainly been able to do in a short period of time.

On his relationship with Florida coach Urban Meyer and are there similarities in the two programs:

SABAN: I don't really know a lot about how Urban does what he does. I have a tremendous amount of respect for him, the program he has put together and the team that he has put together and the coaching job they do. I know they work hard. They do a great job of recruiting. In every dealing that I have had with him, he is absolutely a first-class person and represents our profession with tremendous honesty and integrity and I have a lot of respect for him from that standpoint. I really don't know how he does what he does; I just know he does a very good job of it. I do know this, and get Terry to tell you this story. I'm not sure which job it was or where it was, maybe it was when I became the head coach at Toledo, he was I think a graduate assistant at Ohio State.

When you get a job, you usually have hundreds of people calling you for a job. This is the University of Toledo, so it's not like we were going to Notre Dame or anything. He called the house and he might be able to tell this better, and I know Terry could, because I wasn't really a part of it, and Terry talked to him and didn't know him from Adam's house cat. And when I came home, she said 'this guy named Urban Meyer called and I think you should hire him. I really liked him.' So, Terry throws that up to me every now and then that she is really a good evaluator of coaches that she could talk to a guy for five minutes when we were both a lot younger with less experience and make a determination that he was a good one.

Jim McElwain

Q. Talk about what McElwain brought to this program when he was there. How did you identify him, though, across the country? He hadn't been around for too long.

SABAN: Pat Hill and I coached together at the Cleveland Browns, and Pat Hill was the head coach at Fresno State. I always sort of out there with my ear to the ground about who the best guys are at every position, coordinators, whatever they coach, so that when you have a situation in the future, you can have a list of people that you might be interested in.

Pat had talked very highly about Jim. So when the time came and we needed a coordinator, Jim was one of the guys highest on my list. When I interviewed him, I was very impressed with him as a person as well as a football coach. What I said at the luncheon, which was very true, I had a hard time talking him into coming to Alabama. If you were the offensive coordinator at Fresno State and you could be the offensive coordinator at Alabama, I would have thought that was pretty good, but I had to talk him into doing it. That's how loyal he was and how humble he was, but he did a fabulous job for us.

Q. With Kirby Smart now at Georgia, Jim obviously at Florida, Will at South Carolina, you got to coach against Jim last year in the SEC Championship game, when you go against your former colleagues you spent so much time with, is there extra excitement for you, or is it business as usual?

SABAN: There's a lot of excitement for me because these guys have opportunities and we want to see them do extremely well and the opportunities that they have. I think it reflects favorably on our program and what we've done, and those guys all did a fantastic job for us.

But, when it comes right down to it, when we play each other, even though you have a tremendous amount of respect for them, all they've done for you and the job they've done where they are, and you have that respect because you work with them and you know them really, really well. You also have a tremendous amount of respect for your team now, you know, the players on your team, the work they've done, the coaches on your staff that have worked hard to sort of develop this chemistry.

So your focus is on what do we do to help our group of players, regardless who we're playing against, sort of do their best in that circumstance and situation. I think in every case when I've played against a former assistant, whether Mark at Michigan State or Jim at Florida last year in the SEC Championship game or Will when he was at Florida, the respect has grown each time because of what they've been able to do as head coaches. And makes you proud that they are doing well. But you're also proud that, you know, your current team is doing the best they can do as well.

On the firing of Derek Dooley and Gene Chizik's supposed 'hot-seat' and if it bothers Saban that the profession is becoming a 'what have you done recently':

SABAN: I think it is what it is. There is a lot of attention to what we do. I think there is a high expectation of what we do. Derek Dooley is a good friend. He has been very loyal for seven years of working on our staff and regardless of what he did or didn't do at Tennessee, he is still someone who is a professional colleague and a friend who we would love to help in any way we can. I personally think Gene Chizik has done a really good job. All I know is playing against him, it's always a tough game, they are always well-coached and they are always well-prepared.

That's all I can comment about. I think that sometimes the standard that everybody wants all of us to play to is not something that is a continuum - it's a process that is constantly evolving.

Sometimes when you get a few things that happen that maybe don't go in your favor, it can affect the results that you get - some that you can control and some that you cannot. Whether I like it or not, it is the world that we live in and I fully understand that two years from now, if we don't have continue to have a good team, that I will be in the same seat that other people are in now. It's the nature of the beast in our profession.

Q. Coach, how did Jim McElwain get on your radar before you hired him? What's your recollection of that process?

SABAN: Man, you guys ask some tough questions, man. I'm getting old to where I have a hard time remembering where I was yesterday. I had a question about something that happened in 2007 and now one that happened five, six, seven years ago.

Pat Hill and I coached with at the Cleveland Browns. We coached together at the Cleveland Browns. So I knew the Fresno State offensive coordinator. He had told me that Jim was a really good coach and had done a good job. When we had an opening, I sort of always do a pretty thorough job of trying to look around and see who's available and who we might be able to get to come here and be our offensive coordinator.

Jim was one of those guys, and Pat Hill thought so much of him that I trusted him, and that went a long way. When I met Jim and talked with him and worked with him, we were certainly happy with the decision to have him on our staff.

Q. And what's Jim's best attribute as a coach, do you believe?

SABAN: I just think that he's got a lot of great assets as a coach. He's a great teacher. He's got a really good mind. He's innovative in terms of some of the things he does and some of the problems he creates. I think he coaches with discipline and works hard to get his players to execute things the right way. He's got a good personality, and he's a great competitor. There's a lot of positive attributes there, I think.

Will Muschamp

On what makes Will Muschamp a good coach and how often they have talked:

SABAN: Will is a good coach because he is a great teacher. He is a really hard worker. He has got about as much passion and enthusiasm as anybody that you're ever going to be around. He relates well with the players, and I think the players sort of feed off of his passion and enthusiasm in terms of the way he coaches and what he does. He believes in the fundamental discipline and hard work, commitment. Those types of things that are sort of fundamental to being successful. He has always done a great job. Will and I have a really good relationship. I talk to him on occasion. I don't talk to anybody during the season.

I don't come in and call anybody. I don't talk to any coaches during the season. It's not because I don't like them or don't want to talk to them, but I'm busy trying to do what we are supposed to do. Unless we have some business to discuss its kind of a mutual respect for what we are all trying to get done at this time of the year. We don't really have a lot of time for chit chat, but if there is an issue or a problem that involves college football, sometimes we do talk. In the offseason, we talk quite a bit.

On if Saban sees a lot of himself as a young coach in Will Muschamp:

SABAN: I can't jump up and down on the sidelines any more like he does. I can tell you that. Will probably, of all the guys that we have had on our staff through the years, probably worked the hardest, did the best job, had the most passion, was probably as well liked by the players as anyone. You go from college to pro ball and he actually called defenses in Miami for a year. Those pro players aren't very accepting of a guy, if he hasn't coached in the league before. It didn't take them long to gain full respect and confidence in Will because of the knowledge that he has and how thorough he is. I think that all players really appreciate when you help them play better. He is a good teacher, and he does a great job. It's been so long since I've been a young guy that I can't even remember, but I was a little volatile at the time too. I hope a little less volatile now.

On how much of Saban and Muschamp's similarities are from Saban's influence and how flattering is it to see the similarities:

SABAN: You'd have to ask him who influenced him. I respect him. He did a good job for me. I love the way he coached the players, and that energy and that enthusiasm is something that not everybody on your staff has to have. I think that having people who have different strengths makes a great staff. It is hard to find guys that have that kind of passion and intensity that relate well to everybody in the organization.

You'd have to ask him how I influenced him. I know who influenced me to be the way I am. It started with my parents and my high school coach all the way through George Perles, Bill Belichick and Don James. All of those folks had a tremendous impact on me because when you are growing up, you learn and then those things become your philosophy on how you want to do things. At that time in my career those people were the people who influenced me. Will has been around a lot of really good coaches, and I'm sure that he has taken a little bit from all of them.

On If Will Muschamp has influenced him:

SABAN: I think that just about every coach that you have association with, you learn good things and sometimes you learn maybe that's not how I want to do it. That's never been the case with Will. I learn from all of the coaches that I'm with. Everyone is responsible for a better way. Everyone makes a contribution to make the organization better. Will certainly made it better in a lot of ways, but so have a lot of other good coaches that we have been fortunate enough to have on our staff, and we have several other good ones here with us now. We appreciate all that they do and all of the effort that they put in and all that Will has done for us.

On the gratification of seeing a former coach like Will Muschamp have the success he has had:

SABAN: I think for me, and probably to put it in perspective, you know when one of your children does something that makes you proud. Not that I don't have a tremendous amount of respect for these guys as men and very good character-quality people, who have tremendous work ethic and are very good at what they do and have a tremendous amount of professionalism. I think people can relate to, anybody that has children, that when your children do something that is very good it makes you feel good and proud because of their accomplishment. That's how you feel when coaches on your staff go on and do bigger and better things and have success in what they do. None of those that have, whether its Mark Dantonio at Michigan State, or Jimbo Fisher, or Derek Dooley, or Will Muschamp, I'm really proud and want to see them all do extremely well. We've had to compete against each other before, whether it was Bill Belichick, who I used to work for, who probably feels a little bit that way about me. We're good friends, and you compete and play against each other, but you don't dislike each other and you don't not have the same amount of respect and admiration for each other and want to be helpful to those guys if you can, even though you compete against somebody in that moment in time, you are trying to do the best you can for your team.

Johnny Manziel

On if Johnny Manziel reminds Saban of any former opponents:

SABAN: I've been around longer than most, and most of our players can't relate to this, but this guy reminds me of Doug Flutie. I played against him a long time ago, but he was a really good player and a really good competitor and that's who this guy reminds me of. He can throw it, he's not great big in stature or anything like that, he's extremely quick, he's very instinctive - has a unique ability to extend plays and seems to know when to take-off and run it.

He scrambles and makes plays throwing the ball down the field. He doesn't remind me of Cam Newton or Tim Tebow who were bigger, more physical, very athletic guys; this guy really doesn't run a lot of quarterback runs. He runs quarterback draws, and he runs when it's a pass and everybody gets all spread-out and he scrambles. The other guys were certainly capable of doing that, this is a unique guy in terms of his play-making ability, his size, quickness and speed and ability to make people miss in space.

On trying to prepare for Johnny Manziel:

SABAN: You just have to practice against scrambling. You have to practice scramble rules, matching patterns, trying to contain the guy in the pocket and push the pocket, because he doesn't just run around you - he'll step-up. Sometimes people think you can play that stuff better in zone, I guess we could have an argument about that, you have more eyes looking at him, but they aren't taking the receivers when they start running all over the field, either.

I just think you have to practice against it and create an awareness with your players of how to defend and I think the big thing is don't give them explosive plays when they do it, that's the real key to the drill. We have to put athletic people on the field, this is not a time to have a bunch of guys out there that can play two-gap on the nose and can't move. People have to be athletic and they have to be able to move, playing against this team.

On the pressure put on defensive backs because of Manziel's play-making ability:

SABAN: I think it puts a lot of pressure on the defense. When you match patterns or when you play zone and match a pattern, and all of the sudden you have sort of taken the pattern away and now the guy scrambles and the pattern is not that pattern anymore. Guys have to know what the scramble rules are and play the guy in their area and hopefully relentless pursuit keeps the guy from being able to reset and get a good throw off. I think it's a combination of all those things that are really important to playing against a scrambling quarterback.

Tim Tebow

Q. Wondering if you could disclose who you voted for for quarterback for the all SEC team.

SABAN: I voted for Tim Tebow. I think he's one of the most outstanding leaders I've ever seen in my coaching career. Certainly played fantastic game against us in the SEC championship game last year. I think he might be one of the most outstanding players in our league.

But I also think everybody should have the right to vote for whoever they want, and I don't think they should be criticized for that. It's what a lot of people have fought for in this country for a long time. So I don't understand why anybody would even be interested. But I guess it's somebody trying to create news. I wouldn't point any fingers about that, but...

Q. As somebody who has coached in the NFL, I was wondering what your take is on Tebow's NFL prospects? Do you think he's talented enough to warrant a top-10 pick?

SABAN: Well, you know, I don't think it's fair for me to judge that because I can't really judge who the other guys in the top 10 are. Being involved in the draft before, if you're not involved in the total body of work, it's very difficult to make those kind of predictions.

But I will say this: I think Tim Tebow is an outstanding quarterback, an outstanding leader. I have no questions about his ability to throw the ball. He made some outstanding throws in good coverage in critical times in our game last year in the SEC championship game. So I have a tremendous amount of respect for him as a quarterback, as a leader, as an athlete, in every regard. I think he is a winner. I think he will be a winner in the NFL.

But I think everybody needs to understand that the NFL struggles to evaluate people who don't do in college what they look for guys to do in the pros. And I don't think they should be criticized for that. It's a difficult evaluation when you play a little different kind of offense. I think Florida has a great offense. I think it's very difficult to defend. I think they do a great job of executing it and coaching it. So I'm not being critical.

But it is different. And that makes it more difficult. You know, a general manager sent me a letter saying, How are you learning all the spread quarterbacks, how the dynamics of the critical factors of the quarterback position have changed because this offense has changed, what are you doing differently to evaluate quarterbacks, because we're having a more difficult time evaluating players that play in that offense?

It affects everyone. The quarterback, as well as the left tackle. If somebody told me we don't know how to evaluate this guy because he's never played in a three-point stance because he always plays in a two-point stance because they're no-huddle, and they're always in a spread. So it's every position that is different from what they would like to see because they have a defined prototype they would like to evaluate toward. When you play in a different type of offense, it makes it more difficult to evaluate.

I don't think anybody is disrespecting him, I guess is what I'm trying to say. I think it's just a little more difficult to try to evaluate.

Q. You were involved in a great football game in the SEC championship. That game came down to dominating Florida in the third quarter, but somehow in the fourth quarter Florida was able to shift the momentum. Looking back on that change in momentum, what do you think happened?

SABAN: We had good football players, they had good football players. It was a great competitive venue to see the way they were playing. That was a great football game. It's a great experience to have the opportunity to be a part of it.

But Tim Tebow and the Florida players sort of rose to the occasion and finished the game like you need to. To win a difficult game, especially a championship game. We have a tremendous amount of respect. And it wasn't that our players didn't do it. I mean, Florida didn't win the game on our lack of execution. They won it because they executed and did the things they had to do to win. That's a compliment to them. It's not a disrespect to our players, because I'm not ashamed for a minute the way we competed in the game and the way we tried to finish the game. They made the plays they needed to make.

That's how you really would like to win games, you know, on your execution, not the other team's lack of it. That's why that's a great game, because both teams competed so tremendously for 60 minutes in the game.

Cam Newton

On how to defend Cam Newton:

SABAN: He's a great athlete, there's no doubt about that. You have to do a great job of tackling. He's a big guy. He's got long arms. He's got a good stiff arm. He's really good at changing direction and has deceptive speed. I think when they spread you out on the field and he scrambles or even when he's running one of his set running plays, you have to do a good job of tackling; you have to a good job of leveraging and tackling. That's what great players do; they make themselves hard to tackle and he's certainly one of those guys.

On Cam Newton compared to Tim Tebow:

SABAN: Both guys are great players and were great players for their team. They certainly impact the game. Even though there are some similarities in some of the plays that they run, their styles are completely different in how they do those things. It's not to say that one is better than the other, it's just that they're different. Cam's very athletic, deceptive, makes people miss, changes direction, and plays with toughness - he'll put his head down on you, too. But I don't like to compare players. They're both very, very good players, but a different style, even though they were both effective runners.

4
COLLEGE FOOTBALL

On the parity in college football and national champions rarely being undefeated these days:

SABAN: I think, that from a players perspective, 14 games in a season - especially when you play in a league like our league where there are six teams in the top 20 or 25, and on many occasions there are more than that, there's actually five teams in our league that are in the top 20, that speaks to parity. I think from a players perspective, the consistency in performance is the most difficult thing to try to generate with your team all the time, especially when you play multiple good teams which means that you can't just get up for one or two games during the season, you have to play just about every week because you're playing a really strong opponent.

That takes a lot of maturity, it takes a lot of commitment from the players and they're at an age where sometimes that's very challenging, and I think that's why sometimes you don't know for sure what you're going to get from week-to-week in college football. I'm not talking about our team; I'm talking about all the teams in the country. When good teams play, even though one team is favored, there are still good teams playing but somebody has to be favored, but when Michigan State loses to Iowa is that really an upset or is that just two good teams playing? I think anybody that is in the top 25 is very capable, and I don't think there is that great deviation between good teams that you can really sit there and say this team should dominate that team. There are a few teams like that most of the time. It seems like Oregon and Auburn are the two teams that have been able to do that most consistently so far this year, but other than that, all the rest of us that have what you would classify as at least a good team have played a lot of good teams and struggled to get that all the time.

On the importance of tradition of the Alabama-Tennessee rivalry as a coach:

SABAN: Well, every game is important. I think to understand what's important to the people, the institution and the tradition you represent. Like I tell our coaches all the time, I can take bad news. I can take good news. I hate surprises. So to me, if you're working here, you ought to do everything you can do not to present me with a surprise, right? It's knowledge of the situation and circumstances. I think, in our position, we have to have knowledge of the situation and circumstance that we are in. Every game is important, no game any more important than the other game. They all have a significant impact on the outcome of the season, whether you're going to have a chance to go to the SEC Championship game or whatever you want to talk about, this game is no different than that, but, at the same time, we understand the importance to our fans with the traditions of our school the importance of rivalry games and they are important because of that.

Q. Coach, you have a lot of NFL experience, of course, and we've seen a rash the last couple years of even some good NFL players stepping away from the game maybe a couple years early. Do you expect some kind of trickle-down effect to the college game, especially since most of the players you recruit have professional aspirations?

SABAN: I think that's a decision every individual has to make. I think that in all that we do, everyone comes to a point, a station in their life, where they look for new challenges or want to do something different, or maybe they are a little tired and not as motivated.

I think that the thing that I respect is some of these players that you speak of have been very dominant players, and the level of commitment that it takes, the work that it takes, the year round sort of commitment that you have to have to play at the highest level and be an outstanding player on a consistent basis, it can, you know, get a little bit sort of difficult to sustain that, and I think it speaks volumes for somebody who realizes when maybe they are not as motivated as before and their pride and performance would not allow them to do something that they don't feel like they can give their very best to do.

So, do I think there's going to be some trickle-down effect? Most of the players that we're dealing with in college are aspiring to develop careers. You know, they are still developing personal characteristics that can help them be successful. They're aspiring to develop a career off the field by graduating from school. They're aspiring to develop a career as a football player that maybe they can play in the NFL someday and they want to have success in college.

So, there's some players that as far back as when I played that decide at some point in their college career that it's not worth it to them. And I think that's going to happen and continue to happen. I don't know that it's going to have a direct correlation to players who make that decision based on the station of life they're in and what their motivation is. I think every individual is going to have a little different sort of feel about what works best for them and what they should do.

Q. You talk about wanting guys who get a start on being successful in life. From all the places you've been, what college football does to help guys do that, what any institution can do to help that along.

SABAN: You know, I think that sports is a metaphor of life. Kind of all the things that we talk about -- and I've already talked about them today -- whether it's commitment, dedication, hard work, perseverance, investing your team in something that you believe in and have passion for, whether it's pride in performance to try to be the best you can be at whatever it is you choose to do, whether it's character and discipline to do what you're supposed to do, when you're supposed to do it, when it's supposed to get done, probably all those things are important to everybody on the football team.

I don't care what business you're in, I think all those things are probably important to you being successful in that. So really the ingredients that it takes to be successful don't change from one thing to another. Being a competitor, to be able to be consistent in what you do, not get affected by the bad things that happen and get frustrated where it affects your performance, not being able to deal with success when things go well, let that affect your performance, are also lessons that you can learn as an athlete that also are important in life.

So there's so many things that are important. You know, golf is a metaphor of life. It's about the only thing I can play now because you don't have to run around and do anything, run and jump or do any of that stuff. You hit a good shot, you got to live with it and hit a good one the next time. With my short game, any time I'm inside of 60 yards I'm horrible. So I hit a lot of good drives that come to no fruition for me in terms of positive performance.

I'm a great scrambler, so when I hit a bad shot I usually recover better because I'm in a lot of bad shot zones. But, anyway, I think it's all a metaphor of life. I think there's a lot of lessons to be learned by young people through athletics and playing sports. I think that's why, you know, promoting high school football, young people playing in youth programs is very important, and a responsibility and obligation that we all have.

I was really disappointed when we voted as an SEC coaching group at our SEC meetings about the head coaches coming off the road and recruiting because we're all afraid somebody's talking to somebody or doing something somebody else isn't or whatever.

The number one reason I like to go out in the spring, it's the one time where you can go show the players and the coaches that what they do is important and you're interested enough to be there and watch 'em. I think that's a responsibility and an obligation we all have because it's promoting high school football. We need to do that. That's a part of our responsibility: To promote our game so that we continue to have people participating and learning how to be successful through our game.

Q. This is not so much about this game, but as a defensive coach, a lot has been made of tackling, maybe kind of a lost art with the loss of practice time, maybe even into the pros. Is that a fair assessment? Do you think tackling is not what it was 10, 20 years ago, and if so why?

SABAN: I think the whole culture of how you play defense and how you have to practice defense has changed dramatically with the no-huddle, fast-ball, speed-ball approach.

I think it's more difficult to coach defensive players in practice because what do you practice? Do you practice the fundamentals or do you practice the pace of play?

Until recently we always emphasized the fundamentals. We didn't play very well when the pace of play was faster. This year we tried to put more emphasis on pace of play, and I do think there is a bit of a downside in terms of fundamentals. Tackling is one of the most critical fundamentals of playing defense because the ultimate objective is tackle the guy with the ball.

So when people used to get in a huddle, you used to practice, a player didn't do something, you had time between plays to correct him, show him exactly what he did wrong, tell him exactly how he should have fit the tackle, how he should have leveraged it, or the technique he should have used.

Now I start to run over there to tell a guy that, they're ready to start the next play, they're about ready to run over me...

As Terry said, stay out of there.

But I think you have to find a balance and do both. And I do think that spreading out defensive players, used to be they had two backs in the backfield, two tight ends, a wide out. There were nine guys in close proximity to the ball, so there was not as much space created.

These plays we see now, there is a lot of space created from horizontal and vertical, all right, which is going to stress the defensive player athletically to be able to make the play in space.

Q. Nick, if you could just comment on what your analysts do and maybe the evolution of support staff over your career?

SABAN: Well, you know, we love it that we can have some extra guys around that are young guys that aspire to be coaches, and I think one of the most difficult things about our profession is how do you get experience so that you can grow and develop as a coach. The fact that we can have a few extra guys now to be analysts, to break down film, to do quality control-type work, you know, I think as an entry level that is beneficial to some guys that can move on maybe to be graduate assistants, get on the field and get some coaching experience. Regardless of where they need to start professionally, I think this is a great thing for our profession, to be able to help develop coaches, and I think those guys now have created a role and a niche for themselves that's very important to every program because we all depend on them.

Recruiting

Q. Given the NCAA rules that keep restricting the amount of time that coaches can spend with kids and spend recruiting kids, the amount of face-to-face time, does something need to be done with that because you guys are held accountable if your players go off and do something, yet the NCAA keeps restricting the rules that limit your contact and your ability to impact your players?

SABAN: Well, I do think there's a balance somewhere in that. I do think that, A, you need an opportunity to be able to get to know a recruit well enough and talk to enough people about him to make a good -- our evaluation is about size and speed, athletic ability to play your position, character, intelligence, and attitude.

Well, the character, intelligence, and attitude part of it is more subjective, and you have to be able to do a lot of research relative to people who have associations and time you spend with that particular player getting a feel for what he's like.

When you don't have that, and we don't have it now because the way this whole recruiting calendar has gone, you know, we offer guys when they're juniors. And unless they come and visit our campus, we never have an opportunity to meet them or talk to them or meet their parents or talk to them, to learn what their principles and values are.

You are right, if we ever take someone who embarrasses themselves, their family, and our program, we're responsible for that.

I also feel like we've made a lot of progress, even though we're not allowed to spend a lot of time with the players once we get them on campus. I think a lot of progress has been made through the years relative to programs you can have that can enhance the development of players, whether it's a peer intervention type program where you address behavior issues, whether it's drugs, alcohol, agents, gambling, spiritual development, how you treat the opposite sex, macho man type stuff, that you educate and try to get players to try to respond to and react to a little better and with a little more maturity so you can minimize the issues.

You don't have to do that personally as a coach. You can affect life skills programs, things like that, that can be effective in those areas. So I do feel like we made a tremendous amount of progress in those areas, because just a few years back we didn't have a lot of that kind of stuff.

Q. In a conference that has the ultimate recruiting tool, a 24-hour-a-day network and revenue sharing of more than $31 billion a year, how come you and the other SEC coaches got really upset about satellite camps and Jim Harbaugh, as far as did you all feel threatened as far as recruiting, and what was the reaction to that?

SABAN: I just think that I wasn't all that upset about it. I don't agree with it. I think that we have a recruiting calendar that clearly establishes times when you can be off campus to recruit. That's not a time where you can be off campus to recruit. So we do not feel in our league that it's a time we should be off campus to recruit. So if other people are going to be allowed to do things, then I think it's important that we all have a level playing field. So whatever the decision is about satellite camps, whether I'm for it or against it or the league's for it or against it, I'm more for having the same rules govern the entire Power Five conferences because we're not just playing in our league now, we're playing in a playoff at the end of the season. So the people that play in that playoff should all do it with equal ability to recruit, be it on or off campus or whatever it is. I think in the NFL they do a really good job of everybody has a level playing field, and I think that's the same way that we should sort of try to operate in college football.

Q. Coach, how has the specific cost of attendance offered by your school impacted your recruiting and your program?

SABAN: First of all, I think this is an outstanding thing that we've done to improve a scholarship for a young man, student-athletes in general, to be able to have a little better benefit as a league and as a coach. We've always advocated a little better quality of life for the players relative to what they do for their institutions, and I'm glad to see this. I've not really, in my experience, our experience so far in recruiting -- now, we don't use this as a recruiting tool. We don't talk to players about this. We talk about the value that we create in personal development, in the success that we've had with our players academically and their opportunity to develop a career off the field if they attend the University of Alabama, and the quality of how we've developed players and the success that those players have had individually, from a team standpoint, as well as having an opportunity to have a career at the next level. And we do a lot of career development stuff to help them launch their career when they leave. So those are the things that we sell. So this has not changed our recruiting, and there's not been a lot of questions asked about it. Now, maybe it will have an impact in the future. I don't think that's the intention of cost of attendance. I think it's to improve the quality of the student-athlete's life, not to be used as a recruiting tool.

Q. The players that you recruit and sign typically have dozens and dozens of offers, many of which come with some promises of immediate playing time. What do you tell players who maybe come to expect maybe an offer with playing time, what do you tell them to have them buy into Alabama where there's the potential they could sit one or more years?

SABAN: Well, we've had a significant number of players play early in their career and make an impact as freshmen. I think probably four or five a year, and certainly we've had three or four on this year's team that have done an outstanding job.

I think we try to create and tell everyone that they're going to get an opportunity to play, and I think one of the things that sort of gets created now in recruiting and college football because of all the recruiting services and five-star, four-star and all this, is an expectation that every young man has, which sometimes can be a little bit unrealistic, maybe if you look at football as really a development, mental game.

So sometimes guys are changing positions, sometimes they're playing positions where time and development is critical to them being able to be successful at that position, and every player is different. So we try to get our guys to focus on what do I need to do to be a complete player at my position, and focus on the development of what they need to do, and possibly, you know, where can I be the best player three years from now. I may have more value; where can I develop to be the most successful person, and where do I have the best opportunity to get an education and develop a career off the field, and my development as a player will be evaluated, really if I want to develop a career as a football player, more after three years than after one year.

So those are the things that we try to emphasize to players. I think guys going to college, we care about the person first and their development, and hopefully our program is something that will help them be more successful in life for having been involved in the program, and they'll learn some of the things that are critical to being successful and get an education, develop a career off the field. They all have a lot more days ahead of them when they're not going to play football than when they are, and the fact that we have 29 guys in this game that already have degrees and have one of the highest graduation rates in the country I think is something that I'm proud of as well as the success that our players have had on the field.

Q. Considering the increase in summer camps and some of the upsets we've seen the last few years, have you noticed the talent gap in college football between smaller schools and bigger schools kind of narrowing recently? Have the increase in camps helped that over the last few years?

SABAN: How does the increase of camps help? I mean, I think players get lots of exposure. I think it's great that players get opportunities in camps, but we all have an opportunity to see these players, and I think they all get evaluated. I think one of the critical things is what Dabo said, and this is one of the reasons I hate to see us change the recruiting calendar, have early signing date, because there are a lot of players -- football is a developmental game, so a guy can be a totally different player when he's a senior than he is when he's a sophomore or junior relative to his development. So when we have to all make decisions early on about physical ability, character, intelligence, academics, all these things, it makes it more difficult so you can make more mistakes in recruiting because you don't see a guy that's more mature physically, emotionally, academically in every way that we try to evaluate players. I think the fact that some of these guys have really good senior years, and we've already sort of passed them up, is one of the reasons that some of these other schools get very good players.

But I also think there's an expectation that is very difficult for players to manage. You know, when you go in a game and you're favored, everybody loves the underdog. The underdog has tremendous motivation. Our team was not the underdog one time all year this year. The expectation is always tremendous for -- whether you're going to win this game and by how many points and all that kind of stuff. It really takes a very mature competitor and a very mature team to be able to play to a standard and not be affected by these external factors and expectations, and that's one of the things that I was really pleased with our team this year, was able to do that for 13 games. I do think we were affected a little bit before the

Florida game by external factors, people running around saying you don't have to win this game. We're playing in the SEC Championship game, you don't need to win this game and you still get in a playoff. I've never played in a game I didn't want to win. I've never played in game that wasn't important to win. But I do think that we were affected a little bit by our approach and preparation in that game by that, and hopefully we won't have to deal with that any time soon.

On recruiting against tradition rich-schools:

SABAN: We had a tremendous amount of respect for Michigan when we were there at Michigan State; we also had a tremendous amount of respect for Notre Dame when we were there. One was 56 miles away and the other was 70 miles away. They are very tradition-rich programs and very well coached. I think that our league now in general has a lot of that. We have a tremendous amount of respect for our in-state rivals. A lot of our division rivals are not that far away; we have a tremendous amount of respect for them. We have to sort of compete against them in recruiting as well as on the field. All of those teams are very good teams and very good programs. I think that the focus has to be on what you have to do to be successful and continue to be successful, not really what you did but what you are doing now and how you need to continue to do that to build so that you can maintain some level of consistency. Whichever school you are, I don't think that it creates an advantage unless you work hard to be able to execute the things that you need to do to continue to be good.

On James Carpenter and recruiting junior college players:

SABAN: I think what I usually say when we are recruiting a junior college guy is they only have two years to play. Maybe sometimes they have three and sometimes they have three to play two years. It just depends on the guy. It's best for them if you have a role for them that they can fit into. Now of course it's their responsibility to be able to execute at the level you need them too to take advantage of the opportunity that they have. I think it works better for them when they have a role and they can come in and play because they only have two years. They don't have time to develop. In James Carpenter's case, we anticipated that Smitty would go out for the draft and we felt like it would help us , even though we had some good young players who were developing, if we had a little older mature guy playing left tackle for us. James has worked really hard and Joe Pendry has done a very good job of helping in develop, and he has played well for us in the first two games. So it worked well for us, but it also worked well for him in that he had an opportunity and he's been able to develop and take advantage of it

On how high-profile games affect recruiting:

SABAN: I think exposure affects recruiting as much as anything. Obviously when you do well, I think people recognize that you have a pretty good program and you develop players pretty well. Not only that, but we have a pretty good academic situation, here, in terms of graduation rates and seniors graduating now. All those factor into player development-type things to help people to be successful. We get an opportunity to show them because of some of the exposure that we get. I think all of that is important.

On how two teams from same conference from the same state affects recruiting:

SABAN: It doesn't really affect what we do at all. My approach in recruiting has never been to worry about what the other guy is doing. I have never done that and never will do it. It's always been about our program and this is what we have and don't say bad things about somebody else, and I'll be honest with you, I don't know any bad things about somebody else. I don't know their school. I don't know their program. I know about our school and our program and the things that we do to help our players to be successful as people, student and players and the organization that we try and use here, in terms of resources, to help them launch their career when they leave. I think it's special. I think it's good and I feel in my heart that every guy should want to come to school here, because we have a great program. So, that's no disrespect or negative to anybody else and it never will be. That's what I believe and that's how we recruit. It doesn't really make any difference what anybody else does.

Saban on why the best DB recruits want to come play for him

SABAN: You would almost have to ask them that question, but I do think there is a history of success that has gone along back to Michigan State, LSU, and here. A lot of the players that play in our secondary really have a pretty good success rate at developing a career for themselves in playing at the next level.

If a player is interested in that, that's not what we're here for. We are here for them to develop personally, academically, and athletically. Then they have a chance to do that. I do think that because we play a pro style system in the secondary, maybe we do more things, we teach more things and guys have to learn conceptually how to plug things in. But I also think players are intrigued by that and I also think players are more prepared to do more than and adjust better in a game when you coach them that way.

Saban on moving High School QBs to a different position

SABAN: I do think guys that play quarterback, most of the time, have a bigger-picture understanding of the game, because of what they have to do as a quarterback. Whether it's what the offense is trying to do or what the defense is trying to do.

In most cases, in my experience, the guys that play quarterback that have the physical characteristics have the critical factors to play another position and are fairly instinctive guys that have a pretty good understanding of the overall game.

The first thing is, you look at a guy athletically and say he's a good enough athlete to play someplace. We were fortunate to get Ronnie Harrison to come to our camp early in his career and saw him do things as a defensive back. That convinced us he could be a really good player. He certainly turned out that way.

Scheduling

Q. What kind of philosophy do you have in scheduling non-conference games? Are you going to have input in this?

SABAN: Well, we're going to have input. Our schedule's set for at least 95% of what happens in the next five or six years, I guess. Philosophically, and I know there's a debate and a dilemma on this all the time, but we have a very difficult league. It's tough from top to bottom. If you're going to have success in the league, it's difficult to play a tough out-of-conference schedule.

But maybe it's from being at Michigan State for 10 years. We always played Notre Dame. We always played somebody out of the league in one of our three non-conference games that gave us a national recognition, prominence, whatever you want to call it. I still philosophically believe that's important.

I am hopeful that we can try to find one opponent each year that we can do that. The thing with Florida State this year, even though they have a great program, all that, I think is healthy for the SEC. I think it's healthy for our program at the University of Alabama.

We're trying to work something possibly for next year, then '08 and '09. We do have Georgia Tech in the future, Penn State in the future in some of those years. Philosophically that's what we're trying to do.

One of the things I think would be more beneficial to our league in doing that -- and, again, this is kind of coming from the Big-10 -- we didn't start the Big-10 season until like September 20th, the fourth week of the season.

We played our three non-conference games right off the bat, all right, which I think is an advantage because if you play a good opponent and you don't have success, your team can continue to improve and you can prove in those three games before you come into league play.

Like this year we play one game, and then we play Vanderbilt, Arkansas and Georgia. Later on in the season, when the players are geared into the SEC, we have non-conference games we have to try to play. I think if we change that as a league it would be much more beneficial to all the teams and would benefit us all a little bit and would help scheduling. I think people would be more in tune to playing an opponent early on that was a quality opponent.

But philosophically that's what we're trying to do. I think it's important to kind of get the national exposure. People who have done that give themselves a better opportunity to win and be recognized nationally. With our current system, I think that's important. Now, you got to win those games.

But that's what we're going -- that's philosophically what we're going to try to accomplish.

Q. Understand you favor a nine-game SEC schedule. Would that make it more difficult for this league to win a national championship? How much support do you have from other SEC coaches on a nine-game SEC schedule?

SABAN: You know, here's the priority. Trying to look at this whole thing from a thousand feet rather than looking at it as how it just affects us, my opinion was the number one priority should be that every player at every school have the opportunity to play every SEC school in his career. That's the number one priority.

Now, it doesn't have to be nine games. But what scheduling format gives us an opportunity to do that? So we've always played two teams on the other side plus a fixed opponent. You can do that by playing eight. You could do it by playing nine. Everybody's got a self-absorbed opinion about why we shouldn't do it because maybe they won't get bowl eligible.

People said when we started the SEC championship game that

we'll never be able to win a national championship because we'll play this competitive game at the end of the year, people will get knocked out. The fact of the matter was more people got into the national championship game because of what happened in the SEC championship game than got knocked out.

We're all playing somebody that is a quality opponent outside the league right now. I don't think the difficulty of schedule would be any greater. I think if you're one of the best teams, playing another team in our league, I mean, would just be an opportunity to prove that you are a quality team.

So I don't know if it would or it wouldn't affect it one way or the other. I just look at it that the number one priority should be that every player have the opportunity to play every school in the SEC rather than being so divisional oriented. I think that should be the number one priority in scheduling.

Q. I know you're not in charge of scheduling, but do you at least understand where Les Miles is coming from when he talks about equal paths to the championship in regard to scheduling on the eastside?

SABAN: Yeah, but there can never be an equal path to the championship. Unless everybody plays everybody, that's the only equal path to championship.

Everybody doesn't play everybody in the NFL. You rotate your schedule. We have to rotate the schedule. The things that I think are important in scheduling is, A, I've been over this before, every player plays every team in the SEC in his career. That means you must play at least two teams on the other side.

I have a tremendous amount of respect for the traditions that our fans enjoy, which our Tennessee game is a big game for our fans.

So the only way to do that is play nine games. So if somebody else doesn't have that...

I understand where Les Miles is coming from. I coached at LSU. We played Florida every year, too. So if anybody understands it, I understand it. You understand? All right smiling.

They may not have that same tradition. My question is, is do other coaches understand our circumstance? Do they understand Auburn/Georgia circumstance? Do they understand the other teams in our league that do have rivalries that are cherished by the fans?

Q. I know you're not in charge of scheduling, but do you at least understand where Les Miles is coming from when he talks about equal paths to the championship in regard to scheduling on the eastside?

SABAN: Yeah, but there can never be an equal path to the championship. Unless everybody plays everybody, that's the only equal path to championship.

Everybody doesn't play everybody in the NFL. You rotate your schedule. We have to rotate the schedule. The things that I think are important in scheduling is, A, I've been over this before, every player plays every team in the SEC in his career. That means you must play at least two teams on the other side.

I have a tremendous amount of respect for the traditions that our fans enjoy, which our Tennessee game is a big game for our fans.

So the only way to do that is play nine games. So if somebody else doesn't have that...

I understand where Les Miles is coming from. I coached at LSU. We played Florida every year, too. So if anybody understands it, I understand it. You understand? All right smiling.

They may not have that same tradition. My question is, is do other coaches understand our circumstance? Do they understand

Auburn/Georgia circumstance? Do they understand the other teams in our league that do have rivalries that are cherished by the fans?

Q. You have Chattanooga on your schedule this year. With strength of schedule becoming a component in the future, will you continue to play FCS schools at Alabama?

SABAN: If we can get 10 quality opponents on our schedule-- look, I've said this before, nobody wants to hear this, but I was in the NFL for eight years where every team you played was in the NFL. So if somebody wants to take the leadership and say, Okay, here are the five conferences that are the top conferences, and we're going to play all our games amongst those people, I'd be fine with that. But until somebody says that, it's going to be impossible to schedule all your games with those teams.

So we will have to continue to play some of those games.

Now, do I think that's what the fans want to see? Probably not. It's a great experience for those players that are going to have the opportunity to play at Alabama this year. It's a great experience for them. I'm not trying to take that away from them.

But I think in the world that we live in, it is impossible to schedule more than 10 games with real quality opponents. It's very difficult. It's very difficult from a financial business standpoint because everybody wants to play more home games for business reasons, which means financial reasons. The more games you play with quality opponents, you're going to have to play home and home. So you're going to have less home games.

There's a lot of issues involved in all that. It's not all about just what the coach wants to do. It's about the business of college football.

So I don't feel responsible to have to make that decision, so I don't really feel comfortable answering that question.

Q. It is much easier to stay at home, schedule a game. This is your third trip here. What is it about this game that makes it worth coming instead of staying home?

SABAN: First of all, I think it helps prepare our team for playing in our league, which is very difficult; playing on the road in our league, which is very difficult. I think when you play against a good team, sort of what I just said, it makes you realize what you have to do to play against the good teams in our league, how we need to improve.

So I think there's a lot of benefits to it. I think there's a lot of exposure that we get because we play in these games.

I think playing in these games in 2008, 2009 did as much to kick start our program as anything we ever did because it was game day. In those days it was the only game. We got a tremendous amount of exposure. We played Clemson and Virginia Tech who were ranked teams and were able to beat them both. I really think that helped kick start our program to become what it's become.

Q. I know you're a proponent of adding that extra league game that was not adopted. With the College Football Playoff coming up, how much of strength of schedule, it may hurt the SEC, and do you ever see the SEC going to add that extra league game?

SABAN: I played in the NFL for eight years. We had 32 teams in the league. We all played the 32 teams in the league. I think that we're talking about going to this five conference sort of whatever we're going to call it, big five or whatever it is. I'd be all for playing all of our games against those guys.

You know, it's what the fans want. I mean, we need to be more concerned about the people who support the programs and the university and come and see the games. I mean, those are the most important. But we never think about that. Everybody is worried about whether they're going to qualify to go to a bowl game, all that stuff.

If we made that rule, we'd have 10 SEC games. But I also don't think you should have to win six games to get in a bowl game. This new committee we got, they're picking six games, is that not right? They're picking all the games that are involved in the playoff, six bowls.

I think they should pick everybody like they do in basketball. If you go 5-7, you have a quality schedule, you can still get in a bowl game, rather than somebody trying to manipulate their schedule, go 6-6 so they can get in a bowl game.

I'm all for playing as many good quality games for players, fans and the betterment of our game.

But I think some fundamental changes have to be made before anybody would be interested in that. I know that everybody thinks I'm crazy, but I think that, you know, every player that comes to an SEC school should play every team in the SEC, which means you have to play two or three teams on the other side. Well, you can't expand the conference and not expand the number of games you play to be able to do that.

I'm the only coach that's interested in doing that, so...

People should make those decisions beyond us. They should do it based on what is in the best interest of our league and college football in general.

On out-of-conference scheduling:

SABAN: It's difficult. If you are not willing to go home-and-home with somebody, which if you are playing a neutral site you don't want to go home-at-home in another game, so you have to get teams that will come here and play. What has been very difficult for the next few years is the SEC has to tell us who we are going to play and when before we can go and schedule other games. We are working through that right now, but I like to play teams that are not going to be so different that you are not improving your team against what they are going to face from other teams that you are going to play in-conference, if that makes sense. Playing Georgia Southern last year, that was a good experience for us, that we may have to play an offense some time, but throwing that right in the middle of the season, being so different, that doesn't necessarily. They did a great job, and I have a lot of respect for them and what they do, and it's a great offense, but you are preparing your team for something that is totally foreign to what they are going to see any other time that they play. We like to play against teams that have some carry-over in what we are going to do down the road versus someone else.

Coach Beamer said it would be tougher for Virginia Tech to lose this game and win the national championship than it would be for your teams, do you agree with that?

SABAN: I think that's one of the advantages to playing in a conference like our conference. I think we've had two national champions, when we won at LSU in 2003, we lost a game, I'm talking about SEC schools. Florida lost a game last year. LSU lost two games, the year they won it, a couple of years before that. I don't know that I agree with his part of it. They have a pretty good schedule this year. They play Nebraska and Miami, early in the season, as well as us. I don't know that I agree with that. Any team that has one loss still has a chance to win the national championship and there is evidence that a team with two losses has that potential as well. If there is anything that I dislike about the whole system now, and I have always been a bowl guy.

I've always been a guy that lots of positive reinforcement for a lot of players who get the opportunity to play in a bowl game for their efforts. If there is anything that has created a negative situation in college football, to me, it's the fact that there is only one thing that matters and that's who wins the national championship. I don't think that's fair to all the other good teams in college football, or all the other players who play in college football. It's a pretty significant accomplishment to win the SEC. It's a pretty significant accomplishment to win the ACC. So, if there is a down side to our system right now, that's why I've always been kind of for the plus-one thing, where there are at least four teams involved in this. Maybe it wouldn't be so much that way. Because if you had four teams, there would be one and two losses, would not knock you out of it and a lot more people would be interested and there would be a lot more teams in the end. So now we're talking about the first game of the season, you're out of it. It's horrible. It's a horrible thought for any team to be out of anything for one game.

The Draft Process

Q. Two questions: First, last night immediately following the game
I talked to a 69-year-old man from Albuquerque, New Mexico,
with tears in his eyes. When you're part of something like that
that brings so much emotional joy to people, what's that like? And
the second thing is what would you advise Rolando McClain as far
as his NFL status?

SABAN: Well, first of all, I sort of mentioned the fact that really
probably the thing that gives you the most positive self-gratification
is seeing other people enjoy what's been accomplished, and that's
certainly true for me. I think that our fans, our players, our coaches,
to have the opportunity to experience this at this time, I know it
means a lot to a lot of people because of the passion that they have,
and that's what makes the University of Alabama a unique place.

I think that's always, to me, where a lot of the positive self-
gratification comes. You know, I won't speak to Rolando McClain
specifically, but when we recruit players, whenever we counsel players
about the NFL, I very clearly state to them that when they're eligible
for the draft, if they're first-round draft picks, and we will do
everything we can to find out what their draft status is, that they
certainly have to make a strong consideration from a business
standpoint to consider coming out for the draft.

But I also strongly suggest to those who are not first-round draft
picks that they should stay in school, graduate, and try to become
first-round draft picks. And the reason for this is if you ever look at
the money chart from the first guy picked in the draft to the last, I
mean, the money falls off the table from 1 through 30. If you're the
50th guy picked in the draft and you can make $4 million and maybe
a million and a half of that is guaranteed, if you can be the 15th guy,
you might make $25 million or $20 and eight or ten of it guaranteed,
it would be worth it to stay in school and graduate and make the
extra $20 million. And that's usually from a business perspective what

we try to tell players.

Now, I know there's a lot of other people out there that try to convince them otherwise, and I think that I don't want to speak for the NFL, but this new salary cap thing for next year is going to affect the guys that are picked in the first 10, 12 picks the most, a little bit for probably the next 10, 12 picks and probably not very much thereafter. So I know there's a lot of promotions going on out there through agents that tell guys that if they don't come out for the draft this year, they're going to lose out on a lot of money. Well, there may be 25 or 30 guys that lose some money, but the rest of them are not going to be affected.

Q. Going back to the agents. How would yanking an agent's license for a year hurt that agent since they have so much cash piled up, they could survive professionally? If you ban NFL scouts from the campus, can't they get tape anyway to evaluate?

SABAN: They probably could. But what else can we do? I'm for doing something. I don't think the system as it is right now is very good. I would hate for somebody to suspend me and tell me I can't collect fees in my profession for a year. That would do me a lot of good in terms of straightening out whatever I was doing wrong, so...

If you weren't writing well and they said, hey, we're not paying you for a year because you're not writing with professionalism, that wouldn't have any effect on how you change what you're doing? I think it would have a significant impact on what they do.

Can you say whatever you want, nothing's about money, but I think most everything gets a little bit about money somewhere along the way. If you make these guys do what they're supposed to do or they can't get paid in that profession, it's going to change what this he do. I'd change. I can't speak for what you'd do, but I certainly would.

It's not fair to the good agents. There's a lot of good agents out there that don't do this stuff. They're not out there chasing guys and giving them money and breaking rules and flying them all over the country, sending girls after them, all kind of stuff. They're not breaking the rules. It's unfair to them.

So, you know, I mean, they could fix it. It could get fixed. You have a standard of behavior and conduct that we have as coaches, that you have as professionals in what you do, that they should have as professionals in what they do. If they don't meet that conduct, they can't make a living doing that, it would straighten it out now.

The NFL can do that. We don't need to not let them come to practice to do that. There's already people that don't let them come to practice. I've never had one minute of our practice ever restricted to NFL scouts, anything we do, in benefit of our players. I would absolutely hate to do this. But I would also hope that the NFL and the NFL Players Association would do something about this without us having to do that.

Q. I'm asking this rhetorically, on this agent thing, what is in it for the NFL to change anything? It's a multi-billion dollar industry that has a free flow of players from you every year. I don't know if there's anything you can do to stop them doing what they're doing.

SABAN: It's not really the NFL. It's the NFL PA that has to do something about it. I think they're the ones that control the situation. I know there's a lot of politics involved, especially with the new Collective Bargaining Agreement, that it may be difficult to do.

It's something that is affecting college football in a negative way. It's affecting college football fans. It's affecting a lot of people. It's not in the best interest of the young people that are doing it.

I mean, if these guys are guilty of doing any of these things that they're being investigated about right now, I mean, the consequences are negative for them and their future. They'll probably not get drafted as high as they could have got drafted if they played and participated. So it's not really good for anyone.

I mean, maybe we need to not be so self-absorbed about how it just affects us and the NFL and see how it affects everyone in college football, including the players, and do something about it.

I don't think it's anything but greed that is creating it right now on behalf of the agents. Agents that do this, I hate to say this, but how are they any better than a pimp? I have no respect for people who do that to young people, none. I mean, none. How would you feel if they did it to your child?

Q. You expressed some displeasure with a couple of your players for choosing the NFL. Is it getting harder to convince the guys that aren't sure fire first-round picks to come back or is it a year-by-year thing with certain players?

SABAN: I think as you look at trends, you'd have to say that I think in three years, we went from 53 players to 102 players going out early for the draft. 36 of those players did not even get drafted this year. I think 32 of those guys got drafted in the first or second round.

My philosophy is, look, I'm not disappointed in any players. When they make the decision to go do what they're going to do, we're 100% supportive of them and we want to see them do well. That benefits them, it benefits us. It's what we're all about, all right?

But we do try to give them good advice when it comes to making a business decision about their football career.

What people don't look at is if you're going to be a fifth- or six-round draft pick, they go out early so they get to a second contract faster. There's only a 25% chance you're going to get a second contract. Your chances of making the team are not nearly as good as a first-, second-, or third-round draft pick.

If you stayed in school, you'd have a much better chance of becoming one of those guys by improving, developing and playing more rather than taking that gamble and that risk that you will be able to sustain a career by being not a high draft pick.

Because the financial commitment that a team makes in you by being a first- or second-round draft pick protects you or keeps or tries to develop you. But if you're not, from a business standpoint, you're really looking at a lot of exposure, especially if you can't make the team, all right, because you have no protection.

So we're going to continue to try to do the things that we've done. I know the NFL has expressed, or we read about some rules that we're only going to be allowed to submit, and you need to check this out, but I just read it before I came over here, five players for junior grades because it's getting overwhelming for them. We had 11 last year.

A guy is going to get a first-round grade, a second-round grade or a stay-in-school grade. Look, all these players that went out for the draft, that went out for the draft late, or didn't get drafted, they were potential draft picks next year. They're not in the draft next year. They're not playing college football either.

Q. Coach, I understand a little bit earlier you had some thoughts about the timing of the NFL's system for providing feedback to underclassmen. Could you expand on that a little bit?

SABAN: I just felt like, in our experience last year, our team chemistry from the SEC Championship game to the playoff game was affected by something. I think that to have a December 15th deadline from when a junior can submit for a draft grade and then you get that assessment back sometime right before or right after Christmas, and then you have a playoff game coming up on January 1st or 2nd, and I think it's my obligation as a coach to inform that young man when I get that information because it's his information, it's not my information, to make him aware of that. And we're talking about a young person who has to deal with a lot now. We had six guys in this situation this past year and 11 the year before. So we're trying to get ready for a game, and all of a sudden, a guy finds out he's a first round draft pick or a guy that thought he was a first round draft pick finds out he's not a first round draft pick, and we're trying to get ready to play a playoff game. I think that it would be better not to submit that information to a player until he was finished competing in college. We've moved the draft back. We have not moved the date that a player has to declare back. Now, those who oppose this type thinking would say, well, how would that affect recruiting? We used to play Bowl games on January 1st. Now the championship games on January 11th or 12th, and the 15th is still the day that people have to declare for the draft. So I think a week, ten days would be beneficial, and I think a rule that says you don't get information to players on draft status until after they've completed their college competition would be beneficial.

Q. Nick, what is the process of sitting down with your juniors and helping them make the decisions they need to make? How does that work?

SABAN: Well, basically I let the players sort of decide how they want to manage that. Each and every year we have a meeting after our last game. This year, last game being SEC Championship Game, to decide who wants to submit to the junior committee to see what their draft status would be.

We have an agent education program that we have people involved with their families as well as the players to teach them the things they need to know about making a good business decision about how they should pursue their future. Then I let the players sort of decide how they want to manage it. Do we want to do this now, between now and the bowl game and now and the playoff game or whatever the circumstance is, or do you guys want to sort of postpone it until we get finished playing. Even though we had guys submit paperwork this year because they have to do it by December 18th, everybody chose to postpone it. So we'll have meetings on Wednesday, tomorrow, when we get back, and I'll share the information that we've gathered from teams as well as the junior committee so that everybody has the best chance to make the best business decision that they can for their future.

I really appreciate the maturity that our guys showed this year in terms of staying focused on what was important for the team and putting that first, and I think it worked out really well for us.

Q. Can you explain just what it's like, how hard the decision is in terms of weighing the option of the NFL to try and help people understand what goes into that decision?

SABAN: I think that one thing that we've tried to emphasize with our players philosophically, maybe I should explain this one, Tony asked me the question earlier, is we try to emphasize with our players if you're a first-round draft pick, the business decision is you should go out for the draft. If you're in a position in the draft where you can enhance your value by staying in college, then maybe you shouldn't go out for the draft. We've had a significant number of players, 17, I think, I might be off one or two, and there were only two of those 17 guys, 15 made good decisions about the best business decision for them. And in some cases, Reggie Ragland last year, had a second-round grade. I'm sure he'll be a top-15 pick this year. If you want to do the math on that, that's like maybe $12-, $14-million decision. Mark Barron did it a few years ago. He was a second-round guy, maybe the seventh pick in the draft. That was a $16, $18-million decision, plus he graduated.

So there's a business aspect to making this decision that I've always tried to get our players to make a business decision. I know every player that's a good player on our team has aspirations and goals and wants to play in the NFL. But you can sort of minimize your value if you get antsy and go out for the draft early because now you're going to sign a three- or four-year contract for a lot less money, and you've got to play with that.

And to me, your value and security as an NFL player is based on how much they pay you, because it's the unearned money that they can't get back on the salary cap that gives you security.

Our players have typically made really good decisions about how they can enhance their future by staying in college and making good business decisions about what they do rather than just emotional decisions about I want to play in the NFL. But sometimes that's not the best thing for them to do at that particular time. The NFL is not going to go away. They'll have all those opportunities next year.

On a report surfacing that the NFL Players Association is going to require agents to cooperate fully with NCAA:

SABAN: I don't really know the answers to all those questions. I do think it's a step in the right direction. I think it shows that there is some unified effort with the NCAA, the coaches association, the NFLPA and the NFL to try to create some solutions to something that has become a problem. Anytime you have this many good players suspended for two to four or however many games, it's not good for college football, it's not good for pro football, it's not good for the players, and it's not really good for anything. It is a step in the right direction and hopefully we'll continue to work to have a good group of people putting their heads together to try to figure out other ways that we can come up with even better solutions.

On Terrence Cody's future in the NFL:

I think a lot of these players they sometimes need to understand that they are constantly being evaluated, in terms of what they do, how they and how they manage issues that they have. I think all those things affect their future. I think Terrence could have a very, very bright future if he makes the choices and decisions to manage himself and the kind of football player he wants to be in a positive way. I think he has a tremendous amount of potential and he has a chance to be a very, very successful player, because they do look for players like him, who are difficult to block, who are good interior players and can play a special role on the team and he can certainly do that.

What NFL GM's look for in college prospects

SABAN: We try to get players to understand football is a developmental game. Even though a great expectation is created for them by recruiting rankings … we try to emphasize development, that football is a developmental game. You're going to be a better player three years from now than when you're a freshman. You need to focus on what you can do to be the best player you can be, and that's what we're going to help you do.

All these guys say, 'I want to play in the NFL someday.' Most people don't look at you until you've played for three years, so why don't you focus on what kind of player you're going to be three years from now? Not one general manager as ever asked me, of all the guys that have gone out early, 'How much did the guy play as a freshman?' Not one.

We will give everybody an opportunity to play as a freshman, and we work to develop those guys and have had some give contributions, and they have the same opportunity as every other player. But I don't know a coach in the country that wouldn't say he should play the best players. The players have to respect that as well.

Staff Turnover

Q. Overall, given the success this season, how important do you think it will be to retain as many assistants as possible, and specifically the two coordinators who may get some interest out of this?

SABAN: Right. Well, I'm always happy and interested for our coaches to be able to advance professionally, especially if it's a professional advancement in terms of a guy being a coordinator who can go be a head coach in a situation where he has a chance to be successful. I think not to have that philosophy and attitude for your coaching staff, that's what they work hard for. That's what they want to do. That's what they try to do, and that's what we would like to help them do.

I'm not pleased when guys make lateral moves because it's a little bit human nature to think, like my dad used to say, the grass is always greener on top of the septic tank. You always think it's better someplace else. You kind of let your ego get involved, and you make moves that you shouldn't make that really aren't in your best interest from a career standpoint.

So I'm not happy when guys do that. But anybody on our staff who can move up, we would like to help them do that. It's important to have continuity on your staff, but at the same time, when somebody does leave, new energy and new ideas come to your staff, and that also can be helpful in the development of improving your system.

You know, I think it happened a little bit this past year. I wasn't happy that anybody left, but at the same time the guys that came in did a wonderful job, and their energy and enthusiasm helped our team this year.

Q. Urban was asked about an assistant that might possibly have another opportunity. At this time of year when there's so much at stake, what's the best way to deal with that on your own staff when you have coaches that may be getting interest from other places?

SABAN: Well, first of all, you know we want our coaches to advance. And I think that if we have someone on our staff, it should be their motivation to do a good job to be able to create a better opportunity for themselves.

In other words, if you're a coordinator, you can become a head coach. If you're not a coordinator, you could go someplace and be a coordinator and actually gain more responsibility.

I don't necessarily think that just a move to move sometimes when it's not really an advancement in terms of responsibility is something that you like to see on your staff, because you hope that the people that are there are working to move up the ladder so they can create an opportunity for themselves that will give them an advancement based on their performance and what they achieve and what they do by doing a good job in the job that they're in.

Because the issues and the problems are the same everywhere. So we always want our coaches to be able to do that. We want to help them do it. But at the same time we want them to stay focused on what's best for our team and our players right now and this situation because those are all things that can be managed after the game.

There's a time and place for all those things. And I don't think today's the right day.

Q. It's a tricky time of the year in college football with coaches moving about, but for coaches in your situation who have huge games coming up, how do you balance at this time of the year a member of your staff who might have some interests from another school to have a better job with the needs of your own team?

SABAN: First of all, I think when you're an assistant coach, when I was an assistant coach, you work extremely hard so you can have success in the program and try to follow the process of what you're trying to do to be successful. You invest a lot of time.

But you also have some personal goals and aspirations like a lot of our assistant coaches do and I'm sure Brian's staff does, as well and that's why you work hard to do a good job.

I think those folks have every right to receive positive self-gratification professionally by taking advantage of some opportunity they have created for themselves by doing a good job. And I think it's just a matter of professionalism where you can separate yourself for a day or two, not affect the performance of what you're trying to do at your job, evaluate the circumstance.

Last year Jim McElwain interviewed for the Colorado State job, came back and coached in the National Championship Game, did a phenomenal job, put a great plan together.

I've been in a situation where we are playing in the playoffs in the NFL and had a college job waiting for me. I just think it's a matter of professionalism on the part of the person that is reinforced positively with an opportunity, but also knows the importance of the loyalty to the players and the things that he tried to accomplish with those players and how important it is to finish those things.

Q. And if you don't mind, do you expect to have your full staffs that you have right now in the Bowl games?

SABAN: You know, we can't really-- I can't predict that. I really don't know what's going to happen. We don't really control those situations.

I know we have some very qualified people on our staff that would be very good as head coaches and I think eventually, they are going to create opportunities for themselves. When that happens, I don't know.

I think one thing you don't realize, if one of our coordinators walked in the room with the offensive or defensive team and said, I'm going to become the head coach at wherever, those players would be happy for that person who has worked hard with them and helped them develop as players; and they would be happy for them and their families, that they would have an opportunity to work hard for something they have created for themselves.

So this is not a negative thing, at all. But again, you know, everybody's got to be a professional about it.

Q. Obviously, at this time of year, there are coaching vacancies around college football, some in the SEC, and obviously some of your staff members will be mentioned as candidates for those. Is that any potential distraction? How do you handle that this week?

SABAN: I've got a lot of confidence in our guys that they're certainly committed to our team and doing the things they need to do to help our team be successful, and I think each and every one of them know that, if they are being considered, it's certainly an honor for them, and I certainly want to help them every way I can.

But the better we play in every game that they're responsible for, the better opportunity they have to advance and reach the goals and aspirations they have professionally. But I'm totally confident the guys will do everything they can to help this team play well in this game.

Q. I wanted to just follow up on a question that you got earlier and just you have assistant coaches that are starting to be pursued by other schools. I was interested in whether you had any sort of official policy as to when they could interview other places and maybe whether you advise them to wait after the Championship Game or whenever to when they can kind of start considering those opportunities.

SABAN: We take every one of those situations individually. We don't really say there's a particular policy. I would like for our guys to stay focused on what they're doing here right now. I have no reason to believe that anybody isn't totally focused because for us to play well at whatever they're responsible for is certainly going to be helpful to any opportunities that they can create for themselves.

So it goes without saying. I had this situation. I had already gotten the job at Michigan State when I was with the Cleveland Browns as a defensive coordinator. For the players, for the team, for your own personal pride and professionalism, you want to do a good job of finishing the job that you have right now. I think those values are really, really important, and I think the guys on our staff, I trust that they believe in those as well.

Q. On helping Jim McElwain transition to head coach at Colorado State while still preparing for the National Championship.

SABAN: Look, I learn all these things from other people, and when other people do good things for you, you think that would be a good thing to do for somebody else.

When I was at the Cleveland Browns in 1994 with Bill Belichick and we were going to go to the playoffs as a team, I happened to get the Michigan State job around this time or whatever, but said that I would not leave the team until, you know, we finished the season and were out of the playoffs. We had a very good defensive team and very close to the players.

So Bill and Art Modell set up -- had a person that helped organize all the phone calls coming in so that when I was working as a Cleveland Browns coach, I wouldn't have to deal with all that stuff. And then when I went home at night, they gave me all the people who called, whether they wanted jobs or recruiting issues or whatever it was, and I'd look at it on my way home, maybe I'd look at it in the morning on the way in, and then I'd hand back and say, please do this, they would do it, and I could go focus on what I was doing for the Cleveland Browns.

So we tried to organize a very similar circumstance for Jim and that was very helpful to us. Hopefully it was helpful to him, because he did a really good job and we played really well on offense in the National Championship Game and ended up winning.

The Playoff

Q. What are your thoughts on the College Football Playoff Committee, some of the criteria they've created, like game control?

SABAN: Well, I don't really have an opinion on all that. I don't think anybody would listen to whatever my opinion is.

I think this is what everyone wanted. I do think, and I said this in the very beginning before any of this started, that the BCS had created a criteria of picking the best teams. There were, what, 12, 13, 14, I don't know how many years of experience that went into creating that criteria, that produced at least some number of whatever, that kind of ranked the teams.

Really their failure was because they could only have two teams in the BCS game. When there were three good teams, it created a tremendous controversy. If you have four, the fifth team is always going to create a tremendous controversy.

But I thought as much of that criteria that could be used based on the experience, probably it would have been beneficial because you never got the feeling there was a vote. The polls were taken into consideration, but there was never really a vote.

So I do think this playoff has created a lot of energy, enthusiasm, and is great for the fans. It's great for college football in a lot of ways.

But I also think there's a bit of a downside to it all because not long ago, every game that got played in college was an important game, and every bowl game that got played was an important game.

How many of you can remember you spent all day New Year's Day watching every bowl game? They were all good games with all good teams.

Now, the only game that anybody's interested in is the teams that are in the playoff. I think the downside of that is there's a lot of good football teams out there that have had good seasons, a lot of players. I just love to see people respect all the bowl games and all the teams that have had great seasons, which sometimes I think is not happening now.

Q. You talked earlier about the downside of the playoff. Obviously with the collapse of UAB this season, what is your thought about the whole UAB situation, and what could a playoff system do?

SABAN: You know, I think one of the things that college football does is creates a lot of opportunities for a lot of young people, all right? That's something that I've always really cherished and respected relative to our profession and what we do as coaches in any sport.

So I hate to see those opportunities not exist for players in any program where they chose to go to get an education and have an opportunity to compete in whether it's a football program or any other program.

But saying all that, you know, there's a business aspect to college athletics that maybe really does fit in the university experience. But whether it fits or not, it does exist, it is a reality, and everybody has to make a decision from a business standpoint as to whether it's feasible for them to have a program relative to the cost and the revenue created.

There's two sides of the issue here. It's not for me to judge other than the fact that I love that we can create opportunities for young people to get an education and compete and learn a lot of lessons in life through the competition. I hate to see it go away anyplace. But at the same time I understand the business part of it, as well.

Q. You mentioned the new format and how people want to talk about that, and certainly that's next for you. Does it matter, when you have four teams that are going to be left regardless of the four, who's the No.1 seed, who's the No.4 seed, and so on through the field?

SABAN: My comment the other day at the luncheon was-- and I guess I should say it again-- is I grew up in an era and a time when every game in college football mattered. We didn't have a playoff. They didn't have a true champion. And I understand the interest in that, and it's great for the fans. But that was one of the unique things in college football is that a lot of college football players got a lot of positive self-gratification from going to a Bowl game, whether they won seven games, eight games, nine games, it all mattered.

And everybody sat on New Year's Day and watched how many games that were all important? Those games are not getting the same respect now because we have a Final Four, and that's all that anybody talks about is who's in the Final Four? I couldn't get them to talk about the game today. I mean, I was trying to get ESPN to acknowledge that we had an SEC Championship game today rather than who we're going to play the next time.

I don't really-- you know, we have to have some system evaluation. I thought the BCS did a pretty good job of ranking teams and had a pretty good criteria. I don't think there's enough out there right now to make any kind of judgments about what's happening right now. I just think that our team has done enough that they should be included, and I don't care who you play or how it gets seeded, all the teams are going to be good teams. And there's probably some other really good teams that won't get the opportunity, and that's the part that I hope gets respected in the other Bowl games.

Q. Nick, having gone through the playoff now twice, do you know of any effect that the four weeks between the end of the regular season and the semifinal game has in terms of whether the teams, either your own team or the opponents, have looked different than they did the way they were playing toward the end of the season?

SABAN: I think it's hard to carry the momentum from the end of the season to the game. I think it's almost like a new season, and you almost have to sort of approach it that way, or at least that's what we've tried to do. We've done it successfully and we've done it unsuccessfully so I'm not sure we have the formula exactly right. But if your team plays well, I think you did it correctly. If they didn't, you probably missed something along the way.

Q. Nick, you've now been through the playoff twice, both of its first two years, and you've mentioned in the past a little bit of concern about as exciting as the playoff is, what effect that would have on the other bowl games, TV viewership was really down this year for games like the Rose and the Sugar Bowls. How concerned should college football be about that going forward?

SABAN: There was a couple things I learned from this. That was my concern when we started all this. But I think our players would sort of agree with me on this, that it was really, really difficult after a long season for us to maintain the sort of intensity that we had. I thought our players were really locked in for the Michigan State game, in the first playoff game, and knowing that we were playing an even a better team in Clemson in this game, it was really hard when we came back after that game, after even we took a couple days off, to sort of get re-centered and refocused on playing this game.

So I know that you can say, well, in the NFL they have playoffs, and sometimes you have to play three or four games in the playoffs, but I think professional athletes are a little bit different than college guys that -- these guys gave up their whole sort of vacation from December the whatever it was, 10th, when school was out, until we're going to school tomorrow.

There's quite a bit of sacrifice that gets made, and I think it's a challenging sort of, how do you get a team to maintain the focus that they need to have. I can sit here and say we practiced too much for the game, but yet when I looked out on the field, we had a lot of guys that got tired in the second quarter.

From that perspective -- and I told these guys, and I knew we were struggling psychologically a little bit getting ready for this game. I knew everybody wanted to do it. Everybody was geared up to do it. But I told them, this is a how do you want to be remembered? We always talk about playing 60 minutes, but this is a 60-10 game. It's 60 minutes of the game and then the 10 minutes in the locker room after the game that you remember for the rest of your life, and what you accomplish actually even transcends your life because they put a plaque up that this team won the National Championship, and the 1926 team, who I'm sure most of those players are not around anymore, they still have a legacy.

Now, the accomplishment is significant I guess is what I'm trying to say. But on the other hand, I am concerned about how does a playoff and a bowl system coexist, and how could we make it better if that's possible or get it right. I think it's difficult on the fans, too, as well as I'm sure the players would agree, we go stay in Dallas for a week to play a game, we come home for five days, and we come out here for three or four days to play a game. I mean, that's hard on fans. It's hard on players.

I think it's a great venue. I'm not complaining. But it's just difficult. You don't have that circumstance in the NFL. You play home and away games when you're in the playoffs.

This whole dynamic of how do we keep a healthy bowl system,

which I think is great for college football, it's a lot of positive self-gratification for a lot of players who had a good season, and the national interest that we have in a playoff, which sort of overwhelms the importance of all the other bowl games.

The Rules

Q. Can you talk about the new kickoff rule? Do you think we're trending towards eliminating the kickoff all together? Also the helmet rule.

SABAN: I think all these rules are probably geared towards player safety. I think that's the number one thing we should always evaluate in terms of our game, and rules that we can sort of implement that hopefully don't change the integrity of the game, but enhance the safety of the players.

Obviously with the kickoff being moved up, we'll probably see less kickoff returns. But I think there's some facts out there, you know, we tried to change the three-man wedge because there are some facts out there that support there are maybe more injuries on kickoff and kickoff return than we'd like, so we'd like to try to tweak the rules so we protect the players' safety.

I don't think there's any question about the fact that a player's helmet coming off is not a good thing. It's probably dangerous for the player. I don't care whether it's stylish or whatever it is, the players need to wear their helmet properly, it needs to fit properly, and it's never good when it comes off. I think whatever we can do to sort of manage that toward player safety would be a real positive for our game.

On his thoughts about the taunting rule that can take a touchdown off the scoreboard:

SABAN: I'm not here to evaluate the call, so I don't really have anything to comment about that. Every player knows what the rule is. Every player has been told what the rule is. Every player has been shown what the rule is. We all accepted it as a rule to try and promote sportsmanship in our game, which I think is very, very important, and the players know the consequences of doing these things before they score and after they score, so I don't think somebody else should be blamed for that. I'm not criticizing any players. I'm not evaluating the call. I would not be happy at all if it happened to us, but I would probably more disappointed in the player than in the call. I'm not evaluating LSU's player, or anything else. I'm just telling you about our players because they've all been told what the consequences are, and when they make the choice and decision to do it, they put themselves at risk for those consequences affecting the team, so who should be responsible for that?

On if defensive players understand what they can and cannot do relative to player safety rules:

SABAN: First of all, I think our officials have done a really good job. And it's pretty obvious if I think they're not doing a good job, in most cases, which is something I'm not necessarily proud of, but there's only been a few of those circumstances, so that's a good thing in terms of the job that I think our officials that we've had have done for us. I do think that there's probably a little bit more of people trying to sort of enforce their mojo on other people, if you know what I mean, just by whether it's trash talking or a little extra hit, or a little extra push as if that's going to, some kind of way, give them an advantage. And I think that challenges the officials to control, which it started a little bit in this last game, and I think that they kind of nipped it quickly. Couple of flags, and then it was gone.

We're constantly trying to tell our players that that does not help us win a game. You should never talk to the guy you are playing against. You've got nothing to say to that guy. We should be doing our talking with the way that we play, the effort that we give, the toughness that we play with, how physical we are, the discipline we play with, and you cannot lose your poise. You cannot lose your poise, and that's an issue we need to work on with several of our players that have sort of kind of gotten drawn into this in the last couple games, and they can't do that. It doesn't help us win. And if we get a penalty, then it actually hurts us.

The SEC

Q. If Alabama wins, it'll be four straight for the SEC. The league has always been good. You've been in it twice now. It seems to be peaking right now. Two questions: Is it better now than it was the first time you entered it? I know it wasn't that long ago. And also, why has it gotten so strong?

SABAN: Well, I think the league -- I've always been asked to make comparisons with the SEC and other places that I've been. I think the league is the way it is because of the top to bottom sort of strength in the league. You know, where most leagues have two or three or four good teams, you know, our league seems to have seven, eight or nine or ten sometimes, so therefore each game that you play, if you're not bringing your A game, you have a good shot of not being able to have success. And I think that's what makes the league better.

Difficult to make comparisons between now and then. I think the league was a lot like that then, and it's stayed that way and continued to improve. I think one of the things that sort of sets the SEC out a little bit is the great TV package and the great exposure that we get with having as many as three games on national TV every week, which other conferences don't enjoy that. They're on more regional telecasts. So there's more of a national sort of exposure that really can enhance your recruiting base, and a lot of players in the SEC I think look -- that are being recruited look at it as a conference where there's a lot of good players and a lot of good competition and a lot of good programs and a lot of good coaches, which I would certainly agree with, and a lot of good schools.

The ability to recruit quality players and having quality programs is why the SEC is what it is.

Q. The SEC wins another championship, you win another championship, we asked you about the SEC, but I guess what I want to know is, is there something quantifiable about playing in that conference that gives the SEC team, your team, a benefit when it gets here to play another good team? Is there something that that conference gives you a slight edge over the other good team that you're facing?

SABAN: I don't think there's any question about it. We had some really tough games with-- I think, were there six teams in the top ten at the end of the season, five maybe? I don't know, I thought there were six when we played the SEC Championship game.

So if you're playing those teams, and we didn't play all five of them or six of them or however many there were, but we played a couple, three of them, those kinds of games, that kind of competition, playing against sort of the best, obviously helps you play another good team when you play in a game like this. And I don't even think it's just those teams, I think it's the fact that there's a lot of teams in our division that we had very difficult games with. So it's almost every game that you play in the SEC is a game that you could lose, and you have to be very well prepared for and you have to sort of play with a consistency. You can't play up and down, or you're going to have problems.

And I think all those things really help the consistency and the players to understand and appreciate what it takes to be successful.

On what separates the pass defense in the SEC from other conferences:

SABAN: I think it probably starts with the guys up front. I have always said that I thought the thing that was different about this league was the pass rushers and the cover guys. The combination of those two things were a little bit better than other places. Everybody has good receivers, everybody has good runners, lots of good quarterbacks, but I thought that those two things were something that were a little better in this league, and I think that probably indicates that. If you look at most of the teams that have good pass defense, A, they are able to affect the quarterback because of pass rush. There are three things you have to do to be a successful passing team. You have to protect the quarterback, so the lines have to block. The receivers have to be able to get open and when you throw them the ball, and they have to be able to catch it.

Number three, the quarterback has to execute, make good decisions, process information quickly, get the ball to the right guy at the right time, all that kind of stuff. When you have good pass-rush people, you affect several of those things. If you can cover a little bit, you can disrupt the timing at least, and all those things to me impact your ability to have passing efficiency on offense. I would say that is probably the biggest thing and most of the people that are in that category have some ability to rush and affect the quarterback.

Thoughts on SEC Expansion:

SABAN: Well you know I've made a comment on this before, and I really do feel like we have a lot of people in the SEC, Commissioner Mike Slive and his whole staff, a lot of great administrators at many institutions in the SEC that can really make much, much better decisions and have a much better opinion on this than I can as a coach, especially in game week worrying about the game. I have all the faith, trust and confidence that all the presidents and administrators will make the best possible decision for our league moving ahead. I think if you understand the dynamics of college football and what's happening then you understand that there are teams and programs that could become assets for other conferences based on the circumstance in their particular conference, and I don't necessarily see expansion as a negative thing. People have heard me talk before about the fact I was in the Big Ten when Penn State came in, and there were a lot of naysayers about all that. The fact of the matter is Penn State made the league better and opened up the Big Ten to the East, and it helped us all recruit better in the East because those kids got exposure in the East from Penn State. The east became one of the best recruiting areas for us as a faraway recruiting area at Michigan State whereas before we could never get a player there. I do think there are a whole lot of folks in Texas, and there's a whole lot of good football over there. I do think there would be some assets that a team from Texas would bring to our league. That doesn't mean I'm for or against it. It means I'm for the people who are in positions to make those decisions, to make them. I'm not going to call them. I'm not going to call the president to ask what play to run on third down, so he doesn't have to worry about getting a call from me, or getting my opinion on whether we should expand or not.

I think that we have an outstanding league, and we have an outstanding league because we have a lot of passion in this league for football. I think it's an important part of the Southeast and the culture in the Southeast. I think our league expresses that in the passion that our fans have as well as the good football players that we're able to attract to a lot of our schools and make our league very competitive, top to bottom with a lot of good teams. I think it makes it a great league. I can't really comment on what it's like for someone else to come here and play. Football is football. I think sometimes our style of play may be a little bit different than some other part of the country. That doesn't make it better or worse, I do think there are probably a little better cover people and maybe a little better pass rushers. And I think when you come and play somebody in this league you better be ready for those things.

On how good the SEC has become over the years:

SABAN: I think there are a lot of good players in this league, period. I think the high school football programs in the southeast are really good. I think there a lot of players that develop. There are a lot of good athletes. There is a lot of speed. I think all those things contribute to the kind of players that they look for at the next level. We're fortunate as a league to have some great institutions that can attract those players with the kind of programs we have and the kind competition that we have in the league. Getting those guys to play in this part of the country all makes our league what it is. It goes back to the players. We've done a great job from an SEC standpoint, the commissioner and the entire league, of having a great league in terms of what we do and how we promote it. I think it still comes back to the quality of players, the type of people they are, and that's what people want to see. That's where a lot of the fan interest comes from, and it's really fun to coach because there is great competition and there are a lot of great players.

5

NICK SABAN: HIMSELF

Q. What do you think the biggest misconception is about Nick Saban?

SABAN: I don't know. That's one you should ask my wife. She says I have a huge blind spot. I'm sure you've heard that one, right? What you think you are compared to how you're perceived to be. She said mine's as wide as the Grand Canyon.

It would be hard for me to answer that question. I think she could answer it much better than I do.

I think probably the biggest misconception about me is I've never adapted very well to the position that I'm in. I'm a country boy who grew up in West Virginia and pumped gas from the time he was 10 years old until he graduated from high school. Made a dollar an hour providing service to other people, cleaning windows, checking oil, changing tires. All right?

To me I'm still that way, but maybe sometimes I don't realize that. Sometimes the things I say mean a lot more than what I would intend them to be. Sometimes, because I'm a little bit shy, maybe that's misinterpreted as not being very outgoing. But I try my best, and I'm getting better and I'm trying to improve every day. Anybody out there that can give me any help, I'd welcome it.

Q. Someone who appreciates good defense, I wonder, when you look back at that first game, the caliber of defense that was played, the level of talent on the field, the level of talent we'll see Monday night, where does that rate among two defenses on one field in one game, that talent level that you've been around?

SABAN: Well, I have a lot of respect for those players that play. First of all, I have a tremendous amount of respect for a great competitor.

You know, when Kristen first started dating and those boys came knocking on the door, I go open a door, the first thing I'd ask them is: What do you play? What do you play? I want to know if the guy was a competitor. I wanted to know if he made a commitment, worked and did something that was sort of going to make him somebody that could overcome adversity and do the right things.

Of course, none of them really ever answered me. They were so intimidated so I never got much good information.

But I have a tremendous amount of respect for the quality of players that they have on their defense and certainly a lot of admiration for what our defensive team this year was able to accomplish.

But I don't think in a one-game season, a winner-take-all game, kind of like this game is, that what you've done in the past is necessarily going to affect what happens in the future.

So everybody's going to have to play well in this challenge, in this game, on this day, for every play in this game. Because there's a lot of talented players on the offensive sides, too, that are very capable of making plays.

So we're going to have to go out there and execute and do a good job to play the kind of defense that was played in the first game.

Q. We saw your wife Terry next to you last night, and you guys have been together since back in high school. Just talk about what her support and encouragement means to you personally, and also for your team. They love to call her Ms. Terry. Talk to us a little bit about Ms. Terry.

SABAN: Well, let me say this: I met Ms. Terry when she was in seventh grade at science camp and I was in eighth grade, and we were from different schools. And she did not know what a 1st down was when we first started dating, and there's no doubt in my mind that she thinks she ought to be the head coach at Alabama right now. No doubt. And she is a hell of an assistant, even though she thinks she's the head coach, which when she's around, I always make her think that.

But Terry does a fantastic job, I think, of being very, very supportive, not only in the things that we do, or try to do, in terms of recruiting and getting to know and develop relationships with people that are important to feel comfortable when they come and visit our university and things like that. She does a tremendous job with our Nick's Kids, which is a tremendous community outreach that helps a lot of people in our state and certainly a lot of victims in the tornado. There's a lot of people who support that organization, and she does a wonderful job of all that.

We make a significant contribution to sending I think it's like eight kids a year on first-generation scholarships to the University of Alabama. She sort of does all that.

She's quick to tell me when we're running it too much up the middle, when we're not passing enough, when we don't blitz enough on defense. I get lots of feedback on all those things. So I would say that she's probably as big a part of the program as anyone in terms of her time, her commitment and all the things that she does to serve people in a really positive way that is helpful to us being successful, not only in football but in the community and what we can do to serve other people.

Q. Nick, does doing this over and over take its toll in any way on you, and how long do you feel like you can keep this going?

SABAN: I don't feel like it takes a toll. As long as I enjoy being around players -- I think the self-gratification that people have to understand is I know as fans and I know as people who have interest in the game, the result of the game is really the most significant thing, the most important thing. But I've talked about this before: Perspective of college football is -- I know it's an entertainment business. I get that. I understand that. I know winning is really important. But from a program standpoint, from a philosophy standpoint, helping these young guys develop as people, seeing them have a chance to be more successful in life, seeing them graduate, going to graduation, taking 23 pictures at mid-semester with guys that graduated, having 29 guys playing in this game that already graduated, seeing guys develop the kind of competitive characteristics and work hard to develop physically so they have a chance to play at the next level, see people develop careers, see our institution use the resources it has to help guys launch their careers, I mean, this is what college football is all about. This is the self-gratification that you get from being a college coach.

It's not just winning the game. It's not just winning the championship. It's always the goal as a competitor, but there's a lot more things that are very positive in terms of what you try to do internally in your organization to help people, build relationships, and I think that's the fun part of being a part of a team.

Q. Have you given any thought at all to how long you want to coach? And another question as well, you talk about keeping players -- I assume keeping them focused on what's ahead is the biggest challenge as a coach. How do you do that in yourself when

you've had so much success to keep striving for more?

SABAN: The best way I can describe it is I hate to lose more than I like winning. So this next game is the game we can lose. I'm not love in what we did last week or the week before that or the whole season. The challenge is the next game because that's the game we can lose, and I hate losing more than I like winning.

My motive as a coach is to help put our players in the best possible position to help them be successful in the game. That comes from our preparation, our teaching, our coaching, whether it's physically, psychologically, emotionally, however you want to couch it. That's how I see my job.

I want to win for the players. I want the players to play their best. I want them to feel good and have the self-respect after the game that I played my best game. Whether we win or we lose, I did everything that I could do to make it happen. That's kind of what my goal has always been as a coach is how can I help our players be the best that they can be as players?

Now, to address the other part of it, I love coaching. I love it. I've done it for a long time. I never wanted to be a coach to start with. Don James talked me into being a graduate assistant when I was coming out of college. I didn't want to do it. My wife had another year of school was the only reason I did it, and I've been doing it ever since, and I love it.

But I think we all have fears sometimes. You have to face your fears. When you start getting up there, you say, I wonder how long I'm going to be able to do this. I'm going to do it as long as I feel like I can do a good job of it, and I'm healthy enough to do it. That's always been what I've wanted to do, and as long as I can keep doing it, I'll be happy doing it.

On what keeps him motivated year in and out:

SABAN: Terry reminded me the other day that this is going to be our 40ᵗʰanniversary coming up here in December. She's reminding me already. Because we were married for a year actually before I started coaching, so that's the only way I figured out this is 39 years. I thought it was more like 31 or 32. I enjoy what I do, I really do. I really enjoy coaching the players, teaching the players. I guess it's the competitive spirit of wanting to do things well, of having the kind of pride in your performance where you let someone else get better than you or get ahead of you. I think that it's just a part of who you are. I still enjoy doing this a lot. I'm looking forward to this season, I think our players are as well. It's just exciting.

I don't know what I could be doing this week that could be more exciting than this. I think next week will be the same way. Until that goes away, which I have no idea when that's going happen, but there's no signs of it yet. We enjoy doing it, we love being here. We have lots of challenges in the future, we have lots of challenges on our team right now, we have lots of challenges in the season, but those things are opportunities that are fun and we're excited about the opportunities we have with this team this year and the challenges that this season will bring.

On news with Urban Meyer going to the hospital and do you take precautions when it comes to your health:

SABAN: My motivation is I figure I can work here and take the stress here, or I can retire and go home and work for Terry and take the stress there. So, so far, I've been trying to keep my day job, because I would be working just as hard at home. That's kind of my motivation. I don't think I really feel like I have an out right now, so I'm willing to hang in there. I will say this, I think that college football is a lot better off with people like Urban Meyer in our profession. He is a true professional in what he does. He has done a fantastic job every place he has been and he does it with a lot of dignity and class and professionalism.

We not only have a lot of respect for him as a person, but the wonderful job he has done everywhere he has been, especially at the University of Florida. So, we're also very mindful and concerned that he doesn't have a health issue that will affect his future and our thoughts and prayers are with his family, in terms of making sure that he takes care of himself, so he doesn't have issues in the future, relative to his health.

Q. Two titles in three years. Clearly you're on top of your game. But I'm wondering is there any part of you saying: I'm 60, I've been doing it for 40 years; if you need me, I'll be at the lake? Or does your fire still burn as hot as it did the first time you were a GA?

SABAN: What do you think? When a guy jumps offsides with three minutes to go in a game and you still coach your team like it's the first game of the season, what do you think? I mean, I'm a competitor. I think the real positive self-gratification you get is sort of seeing people maybe perform, accomplish to, become more than even they thought they might be.

And that's sort of why we do this. Not only from a winning the football game standpoint, but from a personal success standpoint, from guys improving their ability maybe to be successful in the future because they graduated from school and they developed a better character about them in terms of what they learned as competitors and football players.

So that's probably the great thing about college football. And we certainly still enjoy that and really cherish the opportunity to be at a place like the University of Alabama where you can attract very good football players and sort of see them develop as people and improve and get better, and that's the part of it that we enjoy.

I really do think that maybe the only thing that's changed about me is winning the game is not enough. It really is not enough. Doing it the right way, sort of trying to set the right example for your players and having people in the organization that are all trying to help and support those players to have an opportunity to be more successful in life, which also includes serving other people, which I think is one of the big things that this team did.

And I'm probably just as proud of our team winning the Disney Spirit Award for their contribution to our community which suffered in the tragedy of the tornado this past year as anything else that they accomplished.

And I think those are important things that serve you well in life. So doing it the right way and seeing guys do the right things.

And we do have a few players who didn't share in this, that had the opportunity to do it, because they didn't make the right choices and decisions. And I feel like we failed those guys.

His Influences

Q. You have a reputation, winner, teacher, demanding. Who influenced you to shape you in the way you are as a coach and as a man?

SABAN: I think first of all my dad was a coach. He was a Pop Warner coach, American Legion baseball coach. He didn't go to college. He had a service station in West Virginia. I worked for him for a dollar an hour for a lot of years. He started out, bought a school bus. We had seven coal mining towns in the county. He would go in each coal mining town, up a hollow somewhere, pick the kids up, take them to practice. Won 26 games in a row, lost one, won 33 more games in a row, beat Joe Montana's team in Western PA when he was at Butler, all this. Took these country kids that didn't have an opportunity to play, taught them how to be successful, how to compete. That certainly is something that has stuck with me as a person and as a player. I played for him. It made me better. The work ethic he taught, the standard of excellence, the integrity that you do things with, the attitude that you carry with you and the character that you carry with you, what you do every day. Those kinds of values affected me.

Don James was my college coach, Kent State. I guess he had as much of as impact on me as anyone in terms of organization, quality of work, being the best you can be. He's the person that got me in coaching. Most people say, When did you decide you wanted to be a coach? I never decided I wanted to be a coach, never, till this day. Coach James, I was playing baseball, he got me off the baseball field and said, I want you to come and be a GA. That's how I started. Being around him made me want to be a coach. I enjoyed doing it because he was very well-organized.

George Perles was an effect on me at Michigan State. There's been a lot of guys that have positive effects. Jerry Glanville. Jerry was a great coach, but I'm not going to leave any tickets for Elvis Presley anywhere. We left him for DB Cooper, who is the guy that was in the airplane in the Northwest somewhere, jumped out with $250,000. Never found him or the money. We left tickets for him when we played Seattle. There were FBI agents at will-call to see if anybody came to pick them up.

You were on the staff with Earl Bruce, as was Coach Meyer. Would you talk about what you took from him? Everybody talks about he's a great teacher, a mentor, as a head football coach. What did you take from him?

SABAN: Well, Earl was certainly an outstanding coach, did a fantastic job from an organizational standpoint. He was very involved with the players. He coached the offense. He knew what was going on in every phase of the operation in the organization. He was a hands-on guy and a very hard worker and excellent recruiter and very well organized, and I think all those things are things that we were able to learn in our experience there, and it certainly has helped us in our development as a coach.

Q. You mentioned a minute ago the things you've learned in the five years. How are you a different coach than you were five years ago?

SABAN: Well, you know, I think as a coach, at least from my standpoint, we learn new things all the time, from new experiences, from other people, from being a good listener in terms of what has helped other people be successful, and how even technology has changed our game to some degree, how we adapt to the players, the team, the personalities, the strengths and weaknesses of what we have to work with. I think all those things probably change you a little bit each year as a coach.

But I don't think the core values of what is important in being successful has changed at all. That's the principles and values in the organization, and the standard that you set for those, and the importance of everybody buying into that. Defining personally, academically and athletically the expectation you have for everyone so that people can be responsible and accountable to that.

I still think that's critical to being successful in any organization.

Q. Could you take a moment and just reflect on your father's influence in your life, and also as it relates to your attention to detail.

SABAN: Well, you know, I had great parents. I was very fortunate growing up, and my dad was a coach but he never went to college. But he coached Pop Warner, American Legion baseball, all those kinds of things. But he also had a service station and a little Dairy Queen restaurant, and I started working at that service station when I was 11 years old pumping gas. But in those days-- notice I said it was a service station; it wasn't a self-serve. So you cleaned the windows, checked the oil, checked the tires, collected the money, gave the change, treated the customers in a certain way. We also greased cars, washed cars.

So the biggest thing that I learned and started to learn at 11 years old was how important it was to do things correctly. There was a standard of excellence, a perfection. If we washed a car, and I hated the navy blue and black cars, because when you wiped them off, the streaks were hard to get out, and if there were any streaks when he came, you had to do it over.

So we learned a lot about work ethic. We learned a lot about having compassion for other people and respecting other people, and we learned about certainly the importance of doing things correctly.

And when I started to play for him in Pop Warner football, he was the same way as a coach; attention to detail, discipline, do things what you're supposed to do, the way you're supposed to do it, when you're supposed to do it, the way it's supposed to get done, all those things that we've all heard about, discipline was engrained in just about everything that we did. And I think that sort of perfectionist type of attitude that my parents instilled sort of made you always strive to be all that you could be, and that's probably still the foundation of the program that we have right now.

We hope that every player in our program has a better opportunity to be more successful in life because he was involved in the program and that we create an atmosphere and environment for his personal development, his academic development and his athletic development that actually is going to enhance his future chances of being successful.

I think Big Nick, as he was called in those days, had a lot to do with that.

Q. Talk a little bit about earlier in your career, some of those coaches who you coached under, Don James, Earle Bruce, how did they impact you? Have you carried stuff through your career that you learned from some of those coaches?

SABAN: Absolutely. Everything that we do, that I know, I've been fortunate to have great mentors and had the opportunity to learn from them. Even my high school coach had a significant impact on me as a person. Don James, especially, who was very successful that I played for in college and started out as a graduate assistant, probably had the biggest influence on me even getting into coaching, which is something that I was not geared up to do. He sort of talked me into being a graduate assistant, and I liked it.

But Don was very well-organized, had great programs for personal development, emphasized all the right things academically. A lot of the same things we do now. The same kind of recruiting organization we did then. You know, every coach that I coached with has had a real impact in how to do things and maybe sometimes how not to do things.

But George Perles, who was a great coach at Michigan State, also at the Pittsburgh Steelers with Chuck Noll, really taught me a lot about developing as a coach. I'm talking about technique of being a good defensive coordinator and a secondary coach, and was great at how he handled people and treated people, was a great recruiter. I learned a lot from him.

Bill Belichick is the other person who, from an organizational standpoint in the NFL in terms of how he runs the program, how he defines the expectation of every part of every person in the organization, probably had as much of an impact as anyone.

So I've been very fortunate to have some really good mentors along the way.

Q. How do you-- when you reflect on your playing career and college playing career how do you describe yourself as a player and what do you think from that experience informed the way you coach?

SABAN: It's been a long time since I was a player. I think that a lot of things that we do in our program is to try to help our players not only be good football players but sort of help them develop the kind of thoughts, habits, priorities, character, making good choices and decisions about what they do, that it's going to help them be a better person in life.

And Don James was my college coach, and that philosophy carries over from when I was a player for him and his staff. And that's something that we've always tried to do in our program, emphasizing education and the value of education and learning how to be the best you can be at whatever you choose to do.

And how to work with other people, togetherness, how to be positive, how to be responsible for your own self-determination in terms of the choices and decisions that you make, and establishing the kind of work ethic that will help you be the best that you can be, well, these are all things that I learned when I was a player. And certainly things that we've tried to implement in our program through the years and hopefully we've helped some of our players not only be successful on the field but have a better opportunity to be more successful in life because of some of the principles and values they learn while they're in our program.

I certainly think it was a benefit to me in terms of my college experience with the coaches and the philosophy that they have and I think it's something that's been helpful to us trying to establish a program that has value for players.

Q. Nick, obviously Bob and Mark could speak to this because they've all had extensive time in Ohio. How, Nick, did the State of Ohio shape your coaching career?

SABAN: Well, I guess I learned how to recruit in the State of Ohio because that was my recruiting area northeast Ohio was my recruiting area for many, many years. Played at Kent State. Had a great mentor and coach in Don James who was a fantastic coach and really cared a lot about his players and shaped my philosophy to this day of trying to help players be more successful in life for having been involved in your program. I started out there, so I think my roots were all there.

Some of the relationships that I developed early in my coaching career certainly were all certainly in that area and I learned a tremendous amount from some of the great mentors that I had. I've been very fortunate. George Perles was the first person at Michigan State to give me the responsibility of being a defensive coordinator. Was involved in rebuilding the program and going to the Rose Bowl there, and that was a great learning experience for me because he had been with Chuck Noll for 11 years and really knew how to win, knew how to handle people and had a great defensive philosophy and certainly helped shape mine.

Then to be able to work for Bill Belichick in Cleveland for four years and knowing a lot of people in Cleveland, that was a great learning experience for me. But because of all the roots that I had from all the time that I coached, Bill was constantly trying to keep the press out so they couldn't see practice. So he'd put them in a little box somewhere in a corner where they wouldn't want to stand. And Linda, who is my secretary now, was Bill's secretary, and I would give her a list of 40 high school coaches all over northeast Ohio who were my buddies that I grew up with and a lot of them were from Youngstown, and they'd get the A-passes, so they'd be right on the sidelines and be able to watch practice.

Then Art would come out and chew Bill's butt out because he's saying who are all these guys over here. They have the good passes and I want the media to get the good passes and they're over there where they can't see. And Belichick would turn around and look at me and say, you see why I'm getting chewed out? Because of you.

So I've always really valued our profession and the people in it, because my high school coach probably affected me as much as anybody, other than my parents, in terms of the things I learned around the coaches and mentors that I had when I was a young player and my college coach Don James.

So these relationships that we have in northeast Ohio have lived on and on and on, and some of them have become great friends and it's because of a coaching profession and the respect that I have for coaches, these guys included.

Q. I know you mentioned the other day you don't like to think about legacies and looking back, but now with five national titles, no coach has won more. That's how many Bear won. Any reflection on where you stand in history?

SABAN: You know, I really haven't thought about it. After somebody asked me that question the other day, the first thing that came to my mind was my first game at Michigan State when we played Nebraska, when Tom Osborne was the coach, and we got beat like 56-7, and I had been in the NFL for four years, and I'm saying, we may never win a game as a college coach. And I remember running across the field and Tom Osborne, I think they won the National Championship the year before and maybe that year, too, he said, you're not as bad as you think. So that's the first thing that comes to my mind.

So I learned a lesson that day, and you know, as long as you do this, it's always about your next play. It's always about the next game. So I've never really ever thought too much about all that. I have a tremendous amount of appreciation for all the players who have played for us, came to our school, bought into our program, did the things that they needed to do to have a chance to experience a championship, whether it was at LSU or the four at Alabama.

That's where most of my appreciation lies is with the players.

Q. From that day against Nebraska, the game has changed dramatically, particularly strategically. You have innovated along with that, but it seems like you have kept a core system in how you recruit, who you recruit, how you coach players, how you relate to players. Why do you believe that's remaining so successful even as so much around the game has changed?

SABAN: Well, you know, my college coach had the same philosophy, and I felt like the things that he did to help me be successful, and I'm talking about Don James, because he taught us a lot of lessons of life, and we want these guys to succeed first of all as people, make the right choices and decisions, the best choices and decisions, have the right thoughts, habits and priorities that help them make those right decisions so they can take advantage of their gifts, first of all, as people. Be more successful in life for having been involved in the program, and all the people in our organization, that's what they work to try to help them do. We want them to all develop a career off the field so that they graduate from school and have a better opportunity to be successful in life, and we have one of the highest graduation rates in the country, and the best in our conference.

And we want to help them develop as football players, and there's a lot of lessons that you can learn on work ethic, overcoming adversity, perseverance, consistency in performance, all kinds of things that come with the games that these guys play.

And I think those things can all be beneficial to help them be more successful in life, and well, as I want to see every guy have an outstanding career.

Sometimes people criticize us and say we're all like business. But I'm going to tell you what, there were more players in the locker room that played for us at Alabama at this game today than I'll bet you anybody has ever had at a game, and that's because they had a great experience at Alabama. They're great ambassadors for the program. We have a tremendous amount of respect for them, and I think they sort of respect the things that they learned.

But we are trying to create value for players so that they can have a better chance to be successful. That's always going to come first to me.

The NFL

Q. Nick, you're a few years removed now from the Dolphins. Reflecting back on that time, how did those years help you as a coach?

SABAN: I think that the NFL was a great experience for me in terms of the football part of it. I mean, you spent a lot of time on football and you don't have to recruit. There's really only two things you do is coach and make your team better and understand the game better. And evaluate players to try to make your team better in terms of who you're going to bring to your team.

So I think those experiences helped tremendously and have helped me learn and grow as a coach and certainly appreciate the opportunity that I had there with Mr. Huizenga and the Dolphins.

Q. Why do you think your talents as a coach might be more suited to the college game than the pro level after your time in the NFL?

SABAN: I like the opportunity that we have here. It's been fantastic. I like the impact that you can have on young people in college in terms of helping them develop personally, academically, as well as athletically, and there's a lot of positive self-gratification of seeing guys mature and develop and develop careers off the field, on the field and seeing them take advantage of opportunities in both those areas.

So I certainly enjoy recruiting and the personal relationships that you have that you develop in recruiting with families as well as the players that are on your team. So it's just been a real positive experience here for us. And our college experience has been great. And we've certainly learned a lot in our pro experiences.

Q. You're now a National Championship coach again. You're likely to be the hot coach in terms of getting offers, phone calls, maybe you have already. I'm just wondering if you could just put it to rest, do you have any desire to return to the NFL at all, or can you without hesitation say that you're staying where you are?

SABAN: Well, you know, how many times do you think I've been asked this question? How many times do you think I've been asked to put it to rest? And I've put it to rest, and you continue to ask it. So I'm going to say it today, that-- you know, I think somewhere along the line you've got to choose. You learn a lot from the experiences of what you've done in the past. I came to the Miami Dolphins, what, eight years ago for the best owner, the best person that I've ever had the opportunity to work for. And in the two years that I was here, had a very, very difficult time thinking that I could impact the organization in the way that I wanted to or the way that I was able to in college, and it was very difficult for me, because there's a lot of parity in the NFL, there's a lot of rules in the NFL.

And people say you can draft the players that you want to draft; you can draft a player that's there when you pick. It might not be the player you need, it might not be the player you want. You've got salary cap issues. We had them here. You've got to have a quarterback. We had a chance to get one here; sort of messed it up.

So I didn't feel like I could impact the team the same way that I can as a college coach in terms of affecting people's lives personally, helping them develop careers by graduating from school, off the field, by helping develop them as football players, and there's a lot of self-gratification in all that, all right.

So I kind of learned through that experience that maybe this is where I belong, and I'm really happy and at peace with all that. So no matter how many times I say that, y'all don't believe it, so I don't even know why I keep talking about it.

His History & Memorable Games

Q. Can you tell us a little bit about the 2001 game between you and Kentucky and talk about the last play specifically.

SABAN: Well, what I remember, most people don't remember the little things and the details of why things happen sometimes, but there was about a 30-mile-an-hour wind that day, and we were fortunate to be able to game manage to get the wind in the fourth quarter by the way the coin toss went and all that stuff. We practice these two plays every Thursday at the end of practice. I forget the exact seconds, but we ran the first play because we could stop the clock and gained about 15 or 20 yards. Hit Michael Clayton on an in-route, then had to go up top.

But the ball sailed and almost went 70 yards in the air because we had a big wind. The Kentucky players actually misjudged the ball. That's what created the tip. Devery Henderson was the key running guy that's supposed to play the tip. And it just worked out that way.

But what I remember the most from it was not that play. I've always been told by mentors, that the worst thing your team can do is play poorly and win. And we played poorly that day and won. And the next week we got our rear-ends kicked in the worst defeat in all the time I was at LSU because of that. That's what I remember the most.

So you didn't expect that answer, did you?

Q. At a time when you're usually wearing the Alabama colors, did it give you pause when you had to put on an LSU coaching shirt knowing the movie would be seen by Alabama fans later on?

SABAN: I'm hopeful all of our fans will understand that the movie is an historical event. When this happened and it occurred, that was the part of history where I was. I think we all try to represent that. Fred Smith called me. I wasn't gonna do this. And out of respect for the Touhy family and the player involved, who we recruited and liked, was glad to see do so well, become a first-round draft pick and graduate and do all the wonderful things that he accomplished, I think it's a great example to college football and college football players, and Ole Miss program that all these things were done. I think it's a wonderful story.

So, you know, it is an historical event. It's no disrespect to anyone. It's no disrespect to LSU or anybody involved at LSU. We have special memories of the times and things we accomplished there. Nothing that can ever happen is going to change that from Terry and I's standpoint. We have a tremendous amount of respect for our fans at the University of Alabama. I have not heard one negative comment about that particular situation because it's not reflective of where I am now.

You know, I was asked last year when we played at LSU to go to Michael Clayton's induction into the Hall of Fame at his high school. I just very simply explained to the players that I'm gonna be here for all of you guys, too. The guys that have played for me in the past, I have a special loyalty to, just like I will have a special loyalty to you. And when you ask me to do these things in the future, regardless of my circumstances professionally, I will be there to support you, just like I was for Michael Clayton and any other player that has played for us in the past.

So no one finds any disrespect in all that. There's certainly none intended to any institution. I think it's just a matter of professionalism that we want to do it in the right way for LSU, as well as the fans at the University of Alabama.

Q. I know coaches, you probably as well, try to keep human emotion out of game planning and actual game situations. But knowing how LSU fans feel about you, where do your human emotions come into play and what are your sentiments towards LSU and playing against them in this game?

SABAN: First of all, this game's not about me. It's not about me for me. Okay? It doesn't define who I am as a person in terms of what we do, how we give, what Nick's Kids does. My wife and I do a lot of things for a lot of people.

We coach for the players. And I'm most concerned about doing a good job for our team and our players and the institution that we represent.

And I have a lot of special memories of my experience here in Louisiana at LSU for what was accomplished in the program here. And no one's ever going to take that way.

And I have a lot of special relationships with a lot of people in Louisiana who appreciate that and have continued to be very good friends and relationships that I really cherish.

So there's really nothing from a personal standpoint in all this for me. It's not about that. It's about a lot of other things that are a lot bigger than me or anything that's ever happened to me.

And I would hope that people can appreciate and respect that. And we understand that we're on the other side now. And I appreciate people's passion for their institution. I appreciate our fans and their passion for our institution, as well as everyone else's. And I respect that. I respect that.

But it's all good.

Q. What do you remember most about your night before the National Championship game in 2003? And can you compare and contrast that to how you're feeling now.

SABAN: 2003? Wow, I was hoping you'd say last year and I might be able to remember.

Let's see, I'm trying to think. When we have night games, we usually go to a movie, and if I remember right-- I am trying to remember the movie. I know last year it was Red Tails, but I don't want to say the wrong movie. But I think the movie, regardless of whether it was the Last Samurai or whatever movie it was, really it was about the honor of-- the message was the honor of being all that you can be, that maybe that might be more important than winning or losing, and that your focus should be on that instead of the outcome.

So I do remember that was the message that we were trying to get our players to focus on in that particular game. It was not necessarily the outcome of the game but what do I have to do to be an effective player, to dominate the guy that I play against in this game for 60 minutes in the game, assuming that that might be the best player I've ever played against. So that was kind of what we were trying to get established in that game, and that's what the focus was. I do remember that.

Q. Winning four National Championships as a coach puts you in very exclusive company with an incredible group of coaches. Can you just talk about the significance of that and being part of that group.

SABAN: You know, I really don't think about it that way. I have a tremendous amount of respect for all the other coaches and what they've been able to accomplish, but while you're in this game, you're always sort of looking for the next challenge of what you have to do to continue to maintain the standard of excellence that you've tried to establish in your organization and try to get people to continue to do the things that they need to do. They can appreciate, as I said before, what they've accomplished, but in appreciating it, you have to understand what it took to accomplish it, and I have a willingness to stay committed to those things.

So that's kind of where my focus is. I appreciate all the players and coaches and folks that have done everything to contribute to the success that we've had in the past. But I also understand that if we're going to continue to do this, it really doesn't help you succeed in the future unless you continue to do the things that you need to do to continue to have that kind of standard of excellence in your program, which is a process that takes a lot of attention and a lot of people's attention and a lot of people's commitment.

Q. You've won four national titles now. A lot of people are starting to compare you with Bear Bryant. What does that mean to you?

SABAN: I don't think I have any reason that anybody should do that. I think Bear Bryant is probably the greatest coach in college football in terms of what he accomplished, what his legacy is.

I think the biggest thing that impacts me is how many peoples' lives he affected in a positive way, players that played for him, because they all come back and say how he affected their life. They don't come back and say, We won a championship in '78, '79, '61, whenever it was. They come back and say how he affected their lives.

There's a lot of Bear Bryant stories that I've learned a lot from, that have made me a better person. I certainly appreciate that, have a tremendous amount of respect for what he accomplished.

There's no way that we have done anything close to what he's done in terms of his consistency over time, how he changed what he did to impact the times. They threw the ball and won. They ran the wishbone and won. I mean, he changed tremendously to do what he needed to do to be successful. I don't think that it would be fair that anyone really be compared to what he was able to accomplish, the way he did it, and how he impacted other people.

Q. I was curious, this is the fourth in seven years for Alabama; what in your opinion is the historical significance of that?

SABAN: Well, I know you all think I'm a little bit crazy, so I'll just go ahead and be crazy. I think that sometimes success can put a distorted perspective on things for you to some degree. I look back to 1998 when we were 4-5 at Michigan State and we were going to Ohio State to play the No. 1 team in the country, if somebody would have told me then that this would have happened, I would have said, I think you're crazy.

But you remember those times, and you remember all the lessons that you learned in terms of developing a process that works for young people to have a chance to be successful, a team dynamic that gives you a chance to be successful, and right now as long as I'm going to continue to do this, I'm going to keep things in perspective and look forward and not backward. I think it's a tremendous accomplishment by a lot of great people, a lot of great coaches and a lot of great players, a lot of whom were at the game last night. That really makes us proud that they're great ambassadors for the university, and always happy to come home.

I can't really talk to you much more about the perspective and the significance of this, because moving forward, it doesn't really mean a lot.

Q. Coach, you mentioned you hated losing. Losing this game in '08, how did that feel '09 and then what was to come? Talk about that part of it.

SABAN: Well, I don't -- all I know is we're on the other end of that. And I haven't thought much about '08 and '09, based on where we are right now, which I think is in '16, and we're trying to look forward, not look back. But I think that players are always more interested in changing, doing the things that they need to do to be successful when things don't go well. It's part of human nature.

I said it earlier. Complacency creates a blatant disregard for doing what's right, and when you don't do things the right way, it affects the process of what you have to do to be successful. It affects the discipline that you need to be able to stay on task to do the things that are going to help you be successful. That's something that we have to make sure that we aren't. When we lose a game, everybody wants to do what they can to fix it, and we haven't done that.

So we have to rely on guys' competitive character, their pride and performance, what they want to accomplish, what they want to do in terms of their legacy as a team. And as I said before, that all gets defined by how we finish. You know, finishing everything is really, really important.

I had an interesting scenario this week that you talk about traditions, you know, Alabama has great football traditions, but then you have Coach Bear Bryant who wears houndstooth, and houndstooth is still a big part of Alabama tradition. Nobody really -- does anybody know what capstone means? Capstone really is the last stone. It means you finished. You built your Temple. You finished. That's what it means. That's what capstone means. That's a part of our tradition at Alabama. We call it the capstone. It's about finishing.

So what is this about? For our team, it's about finishing. So to do everything we can to make our guys understand what it takes to finish against a very, very good team. And it's a challenge because they are a good team.

Q. Coach, I know, again, you don't like looking necessarily at legacy stuff, but this could be, if you guys win two, three more games here, could win your sixth National Title as a coach. Bear Bryant is the only one to do that. What would that mean to you if you thought at all about that?

SABAN: I haven't thought about it. I'm not thinking about it. I'm focusing on what can I do for our players so we have a chance to win the SEC Championship tomorrow, and that's really all I'm focusing on.

I'm really -- regardless of what happens beyond that, it's going to be about the players on this team. They've worked hard. They've done a lot. The coaches and players on this team have worked hard and contributed and deserve all the credit for all the success that this team has created for itself. Hopefully, we can just do enough to help them finish so that they can do something of significance that will define their legacy as a team. We're focused on that one day at a time.

I talked about be where your feet are. I'm right here right now. This is what's important, and this is what we have to focus on.

On the fastest players that he has seen or coached and how the defense is affected when they are preparing:

SABAN: I guess the first guy that comes to mind is Willie Gault when I was coaching at the Houston Oilers. In the NFL, people played off of him 13 or 14 yards. He would just run down the field. He only ran three routes. He ran a nine, he ran a hook and he ran an out route. The guy was a really good player for a long time because everybody was afraid that he would run by them. With Jerry Glanville, we were going to run a bump and run no matter what and we did. We actually jammed the guy a little bit so we slowed him down and made it a little more difficult for him. I think that when you have that kind of speed, especially on the perimeter, that it's so important defensively to keep leverage on the ball. I call it side boards on the defense, so people can't run around you. Even the play that we had last year where Joe Adams catches a screen on this side and ends up going all the way down the other sidelines. Those are the kind of plays that you've got to really guard against. The backside players can't relax either. You've got to press the ball and force the ball with leverage all the time at every position on the field. The backside support guy is just as important sometimes as the front side guy. Most people that you play, that isn't an issue, but with these guys it's an issue.

On previous experiences with hurricane weather:

SABAN: We had a real difficult hurricane situation in Miami. We lost a game because we changed a game that was supposed to be played on Sunday got moved to Friday and didn't get notice of that until Thursday. We always practiced early at 11:00 in the morning. Kansas City was the team we were playing and they didn't practice until 2:00 in the afternoon. Plus they were in a different time zone so they tell us 11:30 that we are playing a game tomorrow and we had already just about finished practice. That was a tough circumstance. The hurricane came and we had to play the next week. We didn't have power for two weeks but the office had a generator so we were able to go business as usual. In one circumstance we didn't have a chance to make an adjustment and the other circumstance where we could adjust it didn't affect our performance at all.

6
DEALING WITH ADVERSITY

Q. You talked about competitive character, your team's ability to withstand some adversities tonight; where does that come from?

SABAN: Well, I think for a long time we tried to start out telling players you got to play for 60 minutes in the game and you never look at the score board. And I think that's hard sometimes for fans to understand because that's exactly how they look at the game. And when you're in the process of being a competitor, you got to play, play to play to play. And everybody's got to win their individual battle on every play. And you can't let the last play good or bad affect the next play.

And I think that's something that our players have bought into. And over a four year period I've never seen a team develop that kind of competitive character that we have so much resiliency to anything that happens in the game and nothing affects -- we got a punt blocked today and it was like, Stuff happens. And they got it on the two yard line. Some people would completely melt down psychologically and it would affect them for the rest of the day.

Q. Coach, you've mentioned quite a bit the success in last year's Bowl game having an effect on how well this team did this year. Do you see this game being the same for next year, especially given the seniors you're going to lose?

SABAN: Well, I think circumstances were different. I made the statement before that change is inevitable, but growth is optional. I think that somewhere during last year's Bowl game, there was a significant number of guys on our team, critical mass of players, maybe more younger players than even seniors at that particular time, that started to want to make a change, that would affect the future.

I think, even though that's a work in progress, I think that change had a significant impact on, you know, the success, the commitment that was made to the success of what this team has been able to accomplish.

I think the circumstances are entirely different now. The challenge of playing a game after you lost a game certainly is something that great teams can do, and do well. That's a challenge for our team. But it's going to be important for this team to remember what they did to have success and be willing to make a commitment to that to duplicate those kinds of efforts in the future, not lose sight of the process, not be satisfied with what was accomplished.

So this is a totally different circumstance to where we were a year ago. And psychologically. We're going to have to have a little different approach to be able to continue to grow and develop the culture of success we want to have and the standard of excellence we're trying to aspire to. Players are going to have to make a different kind of commitment because they can't be satisfied.

We certainly hope they won't be. Our expectation is the demands on them are going to continue to be high. I hope they have the same personal aspirations to continue to improve and get better.

Q. Last year's disappointment of walking off this field with a loss, was that mentioned much this week? Is that something that's been boiling since last December?

SABAN: Well, I think our players learned from their experience last year. Florida's a very good team and we're interested in playing our best football game of the year. And we want each player to play each play in the game like this is my best play I have to play and be responsible on and give effort to and knowing that every play can have an effect and impact on the game.

And hopefully our players learned last year what it takes to win a championship. But these are two good teams playing. And it can be a great football game. And it's probably too bad that somebody has to win and somebody has to lose, based on what everybody's accomplished.

But that's the way it is. And I want our guys to give a championship effort and be champions in the way they go about their effort as a team in terms of their responsibility to execute their attitude and relentless competitive attitude and how they compete in the game, knowing that just like I said in my opening statement, the other team's championship team, too, or they wouldn't be here.

So it's disappointing always to lose and not be successful. But I think our focus is playing our best game of the year.

Q. Nick, the last time you were in the national championship game against Texas, you did a fake punt on the first series. Was that a predesigned play or a Les Miles moment or what that was?

SABAN: To be honest with you, it was probably a mistake, because it didn't work. But the way we went into that game, because they used to uncover the gunners a lot on the punt and nobody would run out and cover him. Sort of daring you to throw the ball to the guy.

Well, we actually made Julio Jones the gunner into the boundary so we could throw the ball to him. And he got hurt on the play before that punt, and we had a freshman who has turned out to be a pretty good player in the meantime, Dre Kirkpatrick, who was in there, and he didn't really run the pass pattern.

So even though it was probably ill-advised, it was automatic to do that the first time they did it, so they wouldn't do it anymore.

And it didn't work. So it was a bad deal all the way around. But sometimes when you do things like that, the players see you being aggressive and maybe it's not as bad as you think.

When I was here at LSU and we played Tennessee in the first championship game, I think it was in 2001, and they were 1 or 2 in the country going to go play in the national championship game, we got behind 14-7 and we were on the 29-yard line with fourth and an inch. I mean an inch.

Now, they had Haynesworth and some big guys playing in the middle. So I said we're going to go for it on our own 29-yard line on fourth and an inch. And we got stuffed. And we sacked them and they kicked a field goal and they got ahead 17-7.

And for the next five minutes of the game I was like in lala-land, like, Why did you do that? That's the dumbest thing you've ever done. My wife even told me: That's the dumbest call I've seen you make since you've been a head coach.

But we were walking off the field after the game, the seniors came up and said: You know, Coach, that was the most important thing you did in the game is when you went for it on fourth down.

I said: Really? They said: Yeah, because when you did that, we really thought we could win. You were being aggressive and you were trying to win, and we were aggressive after that and we ended up winning the game 31-20.

So even sometimes the dumbest things you do, you never know

how people are going to respond to them. And that was one of the dumb ones, and throwing that pass against Texas last year was one of the dumb ones, too. There's many more in between, incidentally.

Q. You've spoken about how your team has exceeded expectations. How has your team been able to overcome that adversity and overcome the struggles of injuries and players that have gone to the NFL or graduated?

SABAN: Well, I think it starts probably with a commitment to the standard of what we want. I think the players understand. We try to define the expectation for every guy in the organization, and I think any successful business probably does that.

So people can be responsible for their own self-determination. They can do their job. When I worked for Bill Belichick we had one sign in the building; it says do your job. Now, he defined what he expected from everybody in the organization, but everybody knew what the expectation was for them, whether they were secretary and personnel, a player; what kind of players we wanted bring to the organization from the personnel department, whatever it was.

And then everybody needs to make a commitment to the standard, be a team player, trust and respect the principles and values of the organization as well as each other, be positive about how you go about your work, and know that it's going to take a tremendous amount of commitment and work to be able to accomplish it.

So I think we start with those types of things and try to get everybody to buy in, and I think they're more prepared to be able to do it when the time comes.

But I think it takes a bit of maturity on the players' part to be able to do that, and we certainly appreciate that, and that's why we've been successful, because of the players' commitment to that.

On if it's easier or more difficult moving on after a loss rather than a win:

SABAN: I don't know that it's easier or more difficult. If you are a competitor nobody likes to lose. That's always difficult. My job is more of a concern on not how I feel, but how do we get the people in the organization to respond the right way and not make me feel better by getting on everybody else, but by trying to get everybody else to do better so that we can learn from the lessons and grow from the lessons, not focused on the past but how this is going to benefit us in the future. How can we gain something from our loss? That's how I try to focus on it, that's the challenge that I have - not to say how disappointed are you, how bad do you feel? I catch it from everybody - my wife's mad, my kids are upset that we lost. I have to be like 'I am too,' but how am I going to affect everybody around me so that we respond the right way to the circumstance that we are in.

Again it's keeping the focus on the vision of what you want to accomplish - not the circumstance. Last week, too many people, too many circumstances, maybe too many interviews, maybe too much 'why am I not playing more?' Could be a lot of things, but that is not the vision of the team. When you have that, you heard Chuck Pagano talk about circumstances and vision - that's what I am talking about. He has a circumstance too. They have one as a team, he has one personally. His vision is to see his daughters grow up and dance at their wedding. So that's the difference, that's what I am trying to do - keep everyone focused on the vision.

On quarterback A.J. McCarron's development and how he handles adversity:

SABAN: I think A.J. has done a good job. I really do. I think that he's played well. I think that as any quarterback, you probably get a little more credit when things go well, and you may get a little bit more blame when things don't go so well. Certainly there's some plays that he has made that have been very, very good plays on a pretty consistent basis all year long, relative to being a first-year starter. And he probably has a few plays out there that he wished he had back. But I'm not sure that there is any player on our team that couldn't say that they didn't make a choice, or a decision, that would like to have back, including me. So all-in-all, I think he has done a very good job of managing the offense, providing leadership for the offense; he's made a lot of good throws - a lot of good throws. We're pleased with the progress that he has made.

On the team getting stronger as the game progresses:

SABAN: Maybe I shouldn't say this, but you know we kind of get everybody's best game. So they usually start out playing about as well as they've played for a while, and you have to kind of work your way through that a little bit. Keep your poise, and just keep on keeping on. I don't think it's all just about how we do it. I think that it's with those guys, this is like the - they even say it; 'we have Alabama signs up all year long. This is a game we point to. This is kind of like a national championship game for us.' I don't mean that in a disrespectful way, but they're out there ready to play. It's our responsibility to get ready to play ourselves. I think that there were a significant number of players that were ready to play. But there were a few who were not quite ready enough, and sort of had to play their way into the kind of intensity that was passed around out there. So we did get better as the game wore on.

On how well the defense has adjusted following the first quarter of games:

SABAN: Well I think there's two parts to that. We really haven't played worth a damn in the first quarter is one way to look at it, and that was certainly the case in this last game, where we gave up half the yards. They didn't change players, and they didn't really change what they were doing, and we did make some adjustments and adaptations to it, and they did do a few things that we probably hadn't practiced a lot, and sometimes, especially in that kind of environment, players don't adjust and adapt, maybe fundamentally like you wish they would. So the one part of that would be that we need to play better in the beginning. And the other part of it, depending on how you want to look at it would be we play better as it goes because we make good adjustments, which we do. They get good information, but I think part of it is how a player thinks when he starts the game.

I think in the more emotional games, players probably are more emotional and think less, which affects mental errors. And high anxiety is not a thing that will help you make good choices and decisions, so that's something that we need to manage a little bit better. I think the way the way you do that is go back to thinking, just think. `What am I supposed to do? What is my assignment? What's the call? How do I execute that? Where should I line up in this formation?' Paying attention to detail, rather than be so anxious to want to make a play or do well, or whatever that you start taking some shortcuts that really don't help you get where you want to go. That takes maturity and you know guys that have confidence and are mature usually do a pretty good job that way.

On how his 2004 LSU team recovered after their first loss off a national championship:

SABAN: 2003, what is it 2010 now? Do you think I can remember this stuff from seven years ago? Kristen was in sixth grade, I don't remember her birthday party either. We've lost a lot of games, most people do. It's unusual to win every game that you play and I think that there are reasons for the loss and you learn from those things. How our players learn the lessons that they learn, from what they have and have not done, we build on the things that they have done and correct the things that they have not done. It's not just about this game.

This is a cumulative effect of what's happened all season in terms of choices that people make, in terms of what they do and how they do it. How they improve what they do. How they develop confidence in what they do. We've got some young guys out there on defense that have been playing for six games now and we quite frankly expect them to start maturing, play with confidence, not make mental errors and be able to make adjustments that we practiced, that's our expectation.

Maybe early in the season we knew that it would take time to develop, but we've had some time to develop them and people need to be accountable to the standard they need to play to. That's the same thing for every position on our team. It all goes back to the psyche of our team, is it what it needs to be? What happened last year means nothing to what happens this year. Have we had the same psychological disposition on this team towards being successful as last year's team? That's a question I'm going to ask.

On forgetting a loss being as easy as forgetting a win:

SABAN: I would hope that it isn't. We have to move on. It's over and done with. There's nothing we can do to get it back. Whatever the players didn't bring is gone forever so we have to learn from it. It's a great lesson to learn from and that's what we're focused on moving forward. Our attention needs to be on Ole Miss and what we can learn from the experiences that we had so that we can improve and get better, no more and no less. If you're a great competitor the loss doesn't just go away.

On what he learned from his team in the adverse situation against Arkansas:

SABAN: I think that you really kind of hope that people can learn lessons and not have to go through horrible experiences to do it. Everybody is sort of willing to change when something bad happens.

A lot of people aren't willing to change when good things are happening. Hopefully we'll have the maturity to be able to learn from the adversity that we had to overcome, some of which we created ourselves, some of which they created with their ability to make plays, but at the same time we have to know that getting it right, doing things right and having a sense of urgency about doing the things the right way is going to help us become a better team, individually and collectively.

I think a lot of our players need to learn that based on the experience that they just had. Now, I'm very proud of the team for keeping their poise and having the composure to come back in the game, to keep grinding, executing and making plays, and some guys came back and made very good plays in the game and made plays when it counted. I think that's a real key for us, but I think what we want to learn is we need to do that all the time.

On a psychological factor being involved when one team has not beaten the other team in a rivalry:

SABAN: It's only a psychological factor if you let it be. It's not to me and it shouldn't be to our players. It's the same old thing, when Notre Dame wears their green shirts. If that's a psychological factor to you, then it's a psychological factor. If green shirts make you play better, then I guess it's a factor, but other than that it's not a factor, unless it's a factor to you and you let affect you. I am sure this game will get decided based on what happens on this field at this time and how the players play. They need to understand that and know that and focus and play well.

On how the freshmen handled a high point and a low point:

SABAN: They don't know what to expect. They didn't know what to expect in the first game. Obviously they made some mistakes and played with some high anxiety relative to it being their first college football game. I think some of those guys made a huge improvement and I think everybody is in a little bit of a different state of psychological flux in terms of where they are. Some guys are managing it well in terms of what their roles are and some guys are frustrated for a good reason - they want to play more. They have to manage their frustration so it doesn't affect their performance.

On Muhammad Ali and becoming a champion:

SABAN: You have to have respect for the commitment and the things he believed in that really changed the world. There's a lot of great athletes, but there's not many that do that and use their notoriety in being a champion to affect the world in a lot of positive ways.

To be a champion is special. It's not the human condition to be as good as you can be. You have to have special characteristics, special traits, which Muhammad Ali certainly did. Champions don't belong on the ground. When he got knocked down in one of the Frazier fights, he got up and finished the fight because his pride, he didn't belong there. That's not who he is. That's not how he wants to be thought of. He got up and finished the fight.

There's also a quote he said, 'I never win the fight inside the lights. I always win it somewhere far away during road work, working to prepare for the fight.' A lot of analogies of philosophical things that he said or things people said about him really reflect what being a champion is all about.

On Losing to Tom Osborne

SABAN: After somebody asked me the other day, the first thing that came to my mind was my first game at Michigan State when we played Nebraska, when Tom Osborne was the coach, and we got beat like 56-7. I had been in the NFL for four years, and I'm saying, we may never win a game as a college coach.

I remember running across the field and Tom Osborne, I think they won the national championship the year before and maybe that year, too, and he said, 'You're not as bad as you think.' So that's the first thing that comes to my mind.

I learned a lesson that day. As long as you do this, it's always about your next play. It's always about the next game. So I've never really ever thought too much about all that. I have a tremendous amount of appreciation for all the players who have played for us, came to our school, bought into our program, did the things that they needed to do to have a chance to experience a championship, whether it was at LSU or the four at Alabama. That's where most of my appreciation lies, is with the players.

7
DEALING WITH SUCCESS

Q. For you personally, has the magnitude of what just happened sunk in or do you think it's going to take a little while for that to sink in?

SABAN: You know, you don't really want to know what I'm thinking. Because what I'm thinking is how are we going to get this done next year. Because this year's accomplishments are next year's expectations. Dealing with success and all that kind of stuff. I'm happy for everybody else. What makes me happy about doing something like this, is that it's made so many people happy and just like winning the SEC Championship, when you look in someone's eyes and see the pride that they have in what you've accomplished, that's the real self-gratification that you get for what we have accomplished here. To see the players' hard work, resiliency, character and how they competed, to see them as happy as they are, and have a life-long accomplishment and a lot of lessons to be learned from this competitive season that they have gone through that hopefully will help them be more successful in their life. Those kind of things to me mean more than whatever. I guess it's something that you can be proud of and take with you forever more, I think when you win these kind of championships you want to win a state championship. When I was in high school, and I got to admit when I go to West Virginia it says 1967 AA state champion. It makes me proud. So I'm going to be proud for a long time about this.

Q. Do your earlier statements mean that you're still going to hold yourself to the 24 hour rule?

SABAN: You know what, when I sat up here after the Sugar Bowl two years ago -- we had 14 football games this year. We have been fortunate to win 13 of them. And my wife, my little girls back there, I don't know where Nicholas is, but I'm going to tell you what, they made a lot of sacrifices for me. Never being there and never being around. So I'm going to enjoy them for a few days, they got to go back to school tomorrow, but they're going to miss tomorrow. Life goes on. So we're going to enjoy this. We're proud of what we accomplished. We're going to have 24 hours to really enjoy what we have done here. And then we're going to go on and try to keep building for the future.

Q. Coach, for what you just talked about, passion and tradition, there is really one level of expectation at Alabama, and that is to win the national championship every year. When you come off a year where you've had a couple of hiccups, I imagine it's easier to get that message across. So how do you keep the message fresh for next year, and have you thought about what that message will be?

SABAN: Absolutely. I think that the most challenging years is you really-- you really have to have a special character about you to not be relieved to some degree by the success that was accomplished.

And obviously we want everyone in the organization to focus on and remember the things that contributed to the success: the commitment, the work ethic, the togetherness we had on the team, the positive energy and attitude.

But that is a little more difficult to get people to resonate toward when they've been successful. I think it's human nature to some degree to sort of get satisfied with what you've accomplished. And it's human nature to some degree to: I accomplished this, now I'm entitled to a little time off, I'm entitled to not having to do what I used to do. And that will not get you where you need to be.

And I think you need to have tremendous leadership and maturity on your team to be able to respond to that in the correct way. And that will certainly be challenging for our group.

But as I mentioned before, we have an outstanding coaching staff. And our team played a great game last night. But Kirby Smart did an outstanding job in making adjustments in the game. He's done a wonderful job with our defensive team all year long, and I certainly hope that everybody realizes all that he's contributed and all the other coaches on our staff has contributed in helping develop the right sort of character and attitude in our players to get this kind of high level of performance on a pretty consistent basis.

Q. What does it say about your group of seniors to look back at their legacy and say they have played in three BCS Championship Games in four years?

SABAN: Well, I think it's a great accomplishment for that group, one of the most successful classes in the history of college football in terms of what they have been a part of, what they have been able to achieve, and probably more specifically, what they have provided a lot of leadership for.

You know, these guys are great team guys. They trust and respect the principles and values of the organization. They have been very positive in how they have affected other people. They have been very responsible for their own self-determination and have the accountability to do the things they needed to do to be successful.

We tried to define those things personally, academically and athletically and give everyone an opportunity to be accountable to it, and they have worked extremely hard, invested their time well and developed a lot of characteristics that are going to help them be more successful in life, which is the ultimate goal of the program.

So I'm really proud of this group, even though it's a small group, there's only nine guys left, several guys have gone out for the draft. But this group has done a phenomenal job and I'm sure they will look back some day and be very proud of what they have been able to accomplish in their career at the University of Alabama.

Q. For the past several days some of your players were asked how to define the word dynasty, and they didn't even want to mention the word.

SABAN: Well, you know, I think to this team, this is about what this team can accomplish. You know, two days after we won the game last year, we had a team meeting, and the first thing I said to this team was, you guys are not the national champions. Some of you played on the National Championship team, but the challenges that this team has are all in front of you in terms of what you're able to accomplish and what you're able to do to sort of set a standard for this team, this year, and what you did last year is not going to have any impact or effect on what you do next year other than make the game that you play against whoever you're playing against a target. You're going to be the target. Everybody is going to bring their A game to beat you because of what you've accomplished.

So you need to be focused on what you need to do to be all you can be as a team, and see what this team can accomplish.

So it's sort of separate. This team is separate from everything that's happened in the past and anything that can happen in the future, and it's sort of precious, present moment of what this team can do.

So I can see why. I wouldn't want to comment about those types of things, and I can see why the players wouldn't, because we're trying to get them to focus on today, this play, this time, the next play, the next quarter, the next game. I mean, that's what we've always tried to do with our players.

I think those are external factors I call them. That's clutter, that when you start thinking about those things, it's very difficult to focus on the things that you need to do to be successful right now.

Q. Some teams go all in, some teams build for the future. Can you just talk about the challenge of having success in the present while always kind of looking towards the future, building towards the future and staying with the process.

SABAN: Well, I think there's no continuum of success. The process begins, but it's ongoing, and in a couple days from now, we have players that may go out for the draft. We have to help them make good decisions about what their future is. We have other players that need to develop that will have new roles on our team next year. We have to recruit character quality players to represent our program.

So the process is ongoing. And if you don't pay attention to that, you're not going to stay up. We got here by five yards. Georgia was five yards away from scoring. So it's a pretty tough league that we play in, and we're going to have to continue to try to improve as a program to have an opportunity to win the SEC Championship or the National Championship ever again because of the competition in our league.

Look, we're really happy, we're really pleased, we're really proud of what we have to do here. We're going to enjoy it for 24 hours or whatever. It's something that you accomplish that you're always proud of, and I'm especially proud of this team because they were able to repeat. That is hard to do. That is very, very hard to do. I mentioned that before. It takes special people who have special character and a special will because you're always fighting yourself when you try to repeat something. The first time you're all charged up, but the second time you have to challenge your will to do it. And these guys did it, and I'm extremely, extremely pleased and happy for them and proud of them.

Q. Not to infringe on your 24 hours, but looking ahead to next year, what does it mean to have a quarterback who's accomplished what AJ has accomplished and come as far, and what is his-- I don't know if he has a ceiling, but what is his potential for next year and what can he do?

SABAN: Well, you know, AJ has gotten better and better every year. I think AJ is a very competitive guy who's an outstanding leader, who affects other people in a positive way. And I think when you watch him and Barrett in the fourth quarter with five minutes to go in the game, you can see what kind of competitors they both are, the kind of respect for each other, and the kind of standard of excellence they're trying to play to. We're always trying to get players to play for 60 minutes and be the best that they can be and not worry about the scoreboard, and I think their reaction to each other was an indication that they're still out there completing and playing like you'd like for them to.

I think AJ, we certainly have to build the team around him. I've talked a lot about it's difficult to play quarterback when you don't have good players around you. I think we should have, God willing and everybody staying healthy, a pretty good receiver corps. We'll have to do some rebuilding in the offensive line. Regardless of what Eddie decides to do, we'll probably still have some pretty decent runners. But I think AJ can be a really good player, maybe the best quarterback in the country next year.

Q. I know this never gets old for you, but why?

SABAN: You know, there's an old Martin Luther King sermon that talks about there's only one guy that I'd let shine my shoes in Montgomery, Alabama, because of the pride he had in the performance of how he shined my shoes. I didn't want anybody else in the world to shine my shoes. And the enjoyment he got that he did a great job for what you did.

And you've probably heard this sermon, and I'm just paraphrasing here, but if you're going to be a street sweeper, be the best street sweeper you can be. Sweep the streets like Michelangelo painted the Sistine Chapel, Like Shakespeare wrote literature. Let them put a sign up right here that says the best street sweeper in the world lives right here. And if you can do that, you do the best there is in life, knowing you did your best to be the best you could be, no matter what you choose to do. That's why.

Because there's no better feeling than knowing you did the best you could be. I don't care if it's what you do, what I do, what the street sweeper does. It really doesn't matter. It's not all about results.

Q. Congratulations, Coach, on winning the SEC West. What do you do to challenge your players so they don't get complacent with so many wins?

SABAN: I think we always try to look forward, and players need to know they're only as good as their last play. Every player is getting evaluated on what he does next. We try to get our players be where their feet are. Do what you can affect today, whether it's a practice in preparation or it is actually a day that we're playing a game.

I think we challenge our players to be all that they can be, as people, as students, and as football players. Complacency is a blatant disregard for doing things correctly, and that's something that we try not to allow to happen because I don't think that helps people be successful.

Regardless of the success we've had this season, the legacy for this team lies in what they do ahead, in this next game and any opportunity they get to play beyond that. That's how this team will get remembered. If Florida wins a Championship, then that's what they'll get remembered for, and our players will have to next year, two years from now, five years from now when they tell their kids, we went undefeated, but we lost the SEC Championship Game.

So if you can't look forward to that challenge -- this team hasn't won a Championship, so they haven't accomplished what other teams have. So there's a lot of challenges left for this team.

On what different things Saban has seen in the offseason from this team compared to 2010:

SABAN: I have said this on several occasions: this team has done everything we asked them to do up to the Michigan game. They didn't really respond the way we wanted last week, but to me an identity is created over an entire season, over a complete body of work. Just like Peyton Manning said, 'one game doesn't make a season.' So, how you progress through the season, how you improve, and what your attitude toward that is really critical to becoming a very good team.

Consistency and performance defines that in a large degree. Now does this team have the maturity to do that? That's what we have to continue working on, not just with the players who don't have a lot of experience, but with the ones who have experience, to drive the leadership, to try to buy into understanding what is important, to progressing through the season. I think I might have said this once before, but the season is a grind. You have to embrace the grind. It's as simple as that; it's the way it is. That takes a lot of determination to be able to do that, but that is really the fact of the matter.

On the team attitude after last year's accomplishments:

SABAN: I think that this team is different from the teams in the past, in a lot of different ways. Everyone is going to say that if the team does not play well, that it is because they feel entitled. I can tell you that from everything that they have done from how they reported to fall camp to conditioning tests, being the top that we have ever had, the work ethic and all that, if this team is not successful it is not because of the character and attitude of the team. It will be because of the lack of experience the team has is certain positions, and they may make too many mistakes to win. It will not get compared that way I am sure, because this team has done everything the right way. Some parts of the team we have good players and good experience, in other parts of the team we will be playing with young players.

How rapidly those guys mature and can execute without making critical errors in the game, if we go play a great game but make one or two critical errors and they make great plays on them we have an entitled team or we have a team that made one or two critical errors that cost them the game. I do not feel like I have seen any part of this team that has not showed that they have the right character and attitude. It is a whole different thing to create consistency in that identity and to be able to have the resiliency to overcome adversity when things don't go your way. That to me is a maturity issue. This team has done what they need to do in order to be prepared for this season and I am pleased with that.

On how the team handles the expectations and hype:

SABAN: I do like the attitude of the team, I like the way the team has approached the season. I think that hopefully they have learned from past experiences that none of these things really matter. That all the things that are important is how we perform, how we play with consistency, the kind of effort, the kind of toughness, the kind of competitive character we have as a team. But all those things are going to be determined by what we do. The preseason stuff is all determined by what we've done in the past, which has nothing to do with what we do in the future. I'm hopeful that the players have learned that by past experience. It's just the way people think, and I don't care what game it is or what league you're playing in, you can't compete that way.

And just because somebody could stand up and say, `Well you beat Penn State last year so you're going to go up there and play, it shouldn't be a problem this year'. They're a better team this year and they're tougher to play up there. So if you think like that, you're going to get beat. So if you think just because you're rated a certain way - and it's flattering, and we appreciate the fact that the program is getting recognized and all that, but it doesn't really mean anything when it comes to the outcome that you get. It's based on what you do, and what you earn, and you have to pay the price for success up front. And you can't hope for it, you've got to do the work, put in the work, go in with the idea that you deserve it but you understand what it takes to earn it.

On the players becoming content:

SABAN: I can't speak for the players. I don't know what they think. If players did think that way, and I'm sure other players would know more than I would about how players think and what they do, that's exactly everything that I'm talking about, exactly what I'm talking about. The focus is not on what you need to do to be successful. It's drinking the Kool-Aid, thinking that just because they say it on ESPN it's so.

Just because you beat Florida 31-6 people start talking about you being the best team in the country. We're not the best team in the country. We had the best team in the country last year and we proved it. We proved it over 14 games. This team hasn't proven anything and that's how I feel about it.

On referring to the coaching 101 manual on how to bring the team back to earth after a big win:

I really don't have that manual, so I really don't know. I've got some of my Dad's old books from Pop Warner League, when we ran the single-wing. There is nothing in there about it. He used to make us run the hill more and bring more leaves down after dark. There was a film about that some place, you know, when I was over in Birmingham speaking. It's pretty authentic, too, except they had to tape the movie in the daytime because the camera wouldn't work at night. When I played we did it after dark, because we practiced until it got dark. Anyway, I think what I talk about all the time is what you try and emphasize to the players. Take care of your business and your business will take care of you.

Focus on what you do and it's about what you do and prepare yourself in practice and the way you need to be the best player that you can be. Do your job for your team and that's going to give us the best chance to be successful. It takes a lot of discipline to do that and it takes a lot of passion, in terms of what you want to accomplish and that's what we continue to do. That same paradox of success is still out there. When you have success the next opportunity you can lose that and you've got to be smart enough to know what it takes to continue to try and improve and perform well.

Remember this, the other guys that we're playing, they've got scholarships too, and they're not bad and they are pretty good. We have a tremendous amount of respect for them because they played every team they've played this year tough and we've only beat them once out of the last three years, which was last year, is that correct? I remember going over there two years ago. I'm like an elephant. I can tell you about how we lost a game in 1984, if you want to know about it.

On how the team should treat a win after a game:

SABAN: What we have always talked about is basically having a 24 hour rule. You play a game you can't necessarily do what a coach does and think about the next team as soon as the last game is over. You enjoy it, you sing the fight song in the locker room and before you get in the shower you start to think about how you are going to match the pattern or attack the other team.

First things first we have got to make the corrections from this game for our players have a chance to improve on the things that they didn't do correctly. I think after 24 hours you need to start forgetting about that game, stop reading the paper and start focusing on the next challenge that you have. It is like what Usain Bolt said. 'I don't really run against the other runners, I run against myself. I prepare to be the best that I can be in every race that I run.' That is really the attitude that you would like every player on your team to have. Go do that every game.

The last game is over and nothing that happened in the last game will help us win the next game and the players need to realize that and understand it. They have to re-center and refocus. Why did the mighty fall - complacency, because people got satisfied and a lot of times that is not helpful to being successful so that is not what we want to be. That is what we have to prove as a team that we can be a consistent team that will compete all the time.

Q. After you won the SEC Championship, Ms. Terry, who knows you better than anybody, said she could already see in your mind already working towards the next game as you were on the podium celebrating. Just curious on the podium last night how soon was your mind moving to what you've got to do next and if you could tell us what you did to celebrate last night.

SABAN: Well, I didn't do much of anything, really. Sat in the room and some of the family and the friends that we had at the game stopped by. And that's celebration enough for me. Again, it was the joy of everyone else that sort of makes you feel good.

But I'm always thinking ahead, anticipating problems. Every success brings a new set of problems. Every success brings a new set of issues, attitude of next year's team, development of the players for next year, issues that you have from a staff standpoint or player standpoint, personnel standpoint, recruiting standpoint. You know, there's really no time to sort of let your guard down because every success brings a new set of issues for everyone. And being able to manage that is what allows you to be successful with more consistency.

Q. You sat here the other day and talked about how there are some players like a Mariano Rivera who have the ability to stay on point and get their message across athletically. I'm wondering if you could share - and I know you talk a lot about it being the players - but why are you able to get your message across? How do you do that?

SABAN: You know, I think, first of all, you have to have the respect of the audience, so you have to have the respect of the players, which I think you get by establishing a good program, and them knowing that you have their best interest in mind personally and their personal development academically and helping them develop a career off the field as well as athletically in terms of helping them be all they can be to see if they can develop a career on the field, and that you have a legitimate interest in using the resources that you have to help them launch a career when they leave, so they can get the best opportunities in life. That's kind of what our program is all about.

So when you make all your choices and decisions based on sort of that mission statement for them, and you hire people who are all committed to that mission statement, I think players respect that, and if they really want to be the best in all those areas, they're really interested in being a part of our program.

So I think it starts with the fact that you've got to gain the respect of the people, knowing that you have their best interest in mind, which is what we kind of pride ourselves or try to pride ourselves in in developing our program.

And then I think that we use a lot of different people that have ways of affecting psychological disposition who have helped us be effective in how we present these things.

I didn't tell the players a story about Mariano Rivera; we showed them a film of that. I showed them a film of Michael Jordan saying everybody thinks the first championship is the hardest, but it's really the next one, because you have to have the will to fight against yourself, to be everything that you can be because you want to be it, because you've already won a championship. And he was able to win six.

So I let those players, those people, affect our players as well as a lot of other people. I mean, we've had a lot of great speakers. We have a personal development program, and I think every one of those people affect our guys in some kind of way to help them make better choices and decisions so that they have a better chance to be successful.

I think it's a combination of all of the above. It's certainly not just what I do.

Q. I know you stay in the moment, but do you ever think about all that you've done?

SABAN: You know, I really don't. I really -- I'm so concerned about this team, these players, what they've worked to accomplish, and what you -- let me try to put it to you this way: At the banquet this year, I gave a speech about thank you, but there's a second part to thank you that no one ever thinks about, that when I was a kid I was thanking my coach or my teacher or whatever, and my dad was picking me up after practice, and he said, you thanked your coach. That was really nice. But there's an IOU that goes with every thank you, which is you owe them your best. You owe your teacher, you owe your coach the best. Well, it's just the opposite to me in terms of what I said to this team, I thanked them for all their hard work, their togetherness, their competitive spirit, all that they were able to accomplish in winning the SEC championship. This was before we had the playoff game. And I owe them. I owe them as the leader of the organization. I owe them our best as coaches and people who can support them to give them the best opportunity to be successful in the next challenge that they have.

So I thanked them for their effort, but I also feel like I owe them. So I've got no time to think about that stuff.

8
CULTURE & PROGRAM MANAGEMENT

Q. The four tenets of your Mission Statement.

SABAN: Our Mission Statement has always been to create an atmosphere and environment for players to be successful first of all as people. Two things, to be successful in life and anything you choose to do, first of all, you have to know what you got to do. You got to make a commitment to it, be dedicated toward it, have some passion for it, work and invest your time in it, stick with it, have some perseverance relative to all of it, and have the kind of character and attitude, thoughts, habits and priorities on a day-to-day basis to make good choices about what you do and don't do so you can realize your dreams. That's the first thing we'd like to try to accomplish with our players and provide leadership for.

The second thing is we want them to get an education. That's the thing that's going to affect the quality of their life more than anything else, something that we want to provide support for relative to facilities and personnel and people who can affect them and help them reach their full potential academically.

We want them to be champions on the football field in terms of developing as players so that they can win a championship someday. And we'd like to use the resource that the institution has at the

University of Alabama to help launch their career and get the best opportunities in life.

That's always been what we try to do as a college football coach, and that's what we'd like to do at the University of Alabama.

Q. Coaches talk about treating players differently to help them overcome their mistakes. Seems likes Urban Meyer is doing that. Can you elaborate on how things have changed in that regard?

SABAN: Well, I think we're all aware that they have changed. If you have children of your own, I think you can probably attest to anyone who has gone through adolescence with someone now knows that they're different.

My kids just flat-out tell me. I mean I didn't have the guts to tell my dad. You know, when I sit and look at my kids and I say, When I was your age, I worked for everything I had. And they just look at me and say, Well, I don't know anybody that does that anymore, Dad. Like you came from outer space.

So it is different. I mean, people grow up different. It's an instant coffee, instant tea, instant self-gratification. Everything is on the Internet. Everything is a picture. Everything is fast. Everything is quick. There's not the same long-term commitment to something and sticking with it and learning from your mistakes. Very few of the things that our young people do now, do they get consequences for? You know, we played checkers when we were growing up. And when you moved the wrong guy, you lost your guy, you got immediate positive or negative self-gratification for it and you learn from that.

You know, my kids push the restart button. They don't even know if they got blown up. I mean so it's different. It's all different.

I'm not saying that that style wouldn't work now. I think with certain people it probably would work. But I think with a lot of players right now, you have to use a little different approach.

But I think that at the end of the day they all want to be good. They all want to reach their full potential. And they all have a willingness that if you can help 'em do that, they have a respect for you, and they'll give you everything they got to do it. That's been my experience.

But I think you have to be a little more flexible sometimes and you have to think outside of the box. That doesn't mean you have to compromise your principles and values in terms of what's important because they respect that more than anything else.

Q. Been varying reports recently of players who either have left or are considering maybe leaving the program. Are you close to the 85 number, do you feel comfortable where that is right now? Would you classify such attrition are normal year-to-year stuff?

SABAN: We have a demanding program. I mean, when I say 'demanding program,' I'm not talking about football. We have a personal development aspect to our program that there's principles and values in the organization relative to developing a successful philosophy, creating the right kind of habits, thoughts, habits and priorities that are going to help you make good decisions, whether it's the Pacific Institute coming in, whether it's a peer intervention program that address behavioral issues, drugs, alcohol, gambling, spiritual development, how to treat the opposite sex, macho man stuff, running your mouth, getting in fights.

Most of the stuff you read about players having issues with come in some of those categories from that personal standpoint. We spend a lot of time trying to develop personalities on our team, characteristics that will help them be more successful, and they'll be more successful in life for having been involved in the program.

It is demanding. We have some players in our program who have not met those demands. We have the same kind of demands academically. We have one of the highest graduation rates in the SEC and in the country, and that's going north for next year because we'll have even more players graduate next year in our program.

But we have a demanding academic system in terms of player requirements, in terms of what they need to do. There are players that don't meet that. And we have the same thing in football. But none of these players are leaving because of the kind of football players they are from our standpoint. There may be some player who leaves because they're disappointed and don't think or don't have the confidence that they can play.

So if we have attrition for any of those areas, and I tell the player, I don't want you to leave, you're a good person in the program, you're a good student. You may be a backup player, but you have to be satisfied with your role on the team 'cause we don't want a player that's disgruntled or negative in terms of our team chemistry for selfish reasons because you're unsatisfied with your role. If you don't think you can achieve that here, I'm supportive in helping you go someplace else.

I don't know how these things get out. But I only address these things when we start fall camp. We still have a couple players who could or couldn't qualify. We have quite a few players who have already enrolled in school. This is from a young player's standpoint. We have some players who will be grayshirted and know they will be grayshirted. And we have some players who are contemplating what their future's gonna be relative to the University of Alabama.

And we have some players who are being suspended, whether it's for behavior or academic reasons, and they won't continue at our school.

Q. I think I've heard other people ask you this question: What do you think is the biggest misconception of not just your personality but maybe your coaching style?

SABAN: Well, I think that, first of all, there's certain things that we think are important to being a champion. And hard work is one of those things, a tremendous commitment to the goals and things that are important to you.

But I also think it's important that people learn how to be responsible for their own self-determination, which is accountability. And to have that in an organization, any organization, you have to define what the expectation is of the people in the organization.

And I find that players and people in our organization really feel good about the fact that they know what the expectation is.

I kind of learned this from Bill Belichick when I was at the Cleveland Browns with him as defensive coordinator, when he was the head coach there, and it was about doing your job and the responsibility and the accountability that goes with that.

But as a leader, make sure you define what that is. And we believe that it's important to be very positive in your approach to doing that, which I think is where the misconception probably starts. You know, you don't have to be negative to do that.

And I think that's probably what our players think. And that we are positive in our approach to what we do. But it's also defined and the expectation is defined for them and we expect them to be responsible to it. And it's really the only way you can have a team, because for people to trust and respect each other, which is important to togetherness on a team, they have to all buy into the same things and you can't have one guy saying, well, he did this but I'm not allowed to do that, because that creates divisiveness which is never going to allow you to have the togetherness that you need to be successful in difficult circumstances.

So those things we believe in, and I think that it's the way we do it that there's a misconception on because it's done in a very positive way.

Q. How confident were you last year that AJ McCarron could carry as much responsibility, play-making responsibility as he did in that game? And having seen him do so well, does that give you an advantage going into this year's game knowing what he's capable of producing?

SABAN: Well, I stop short of any advantages because their players are capable of making plays, too. But I think the fact that we did have a lot of faith, trust and confidence in AJ last year in the game, and that's something that I'm not sure we showed throughout the course of the year, but felt like we needed to have that kind of trust in him to be able to attack LSU's defense at the time. That was who we were playing last year, which was a very good defense. And he certainly did an outstanding job in executing that.

And I think that he's playing against a very, very good defensive team this year, and I think his ability to make good choices and decisions is going to be a critical factor in how well we do offensively, and he has a little more experience in all that. So you could say because he has that experience, there's more of an expectation that he could do that. But it is something that he has to go out and do and make happen against a very, very good defensive team.

And I don't think the burden is just on him. I think quarterback is a very difficult position to play if the players around you don't play well. So it's up to the offensive line, the tight ends, the wide receivers have to run good routes, they have to get open, they have to catch the ball when it gets delivered to them, we have to pass protect, he has to make good choices and decisions. So all these things become critical factors in being successful offensively.

So people playing well around AJ is going to be a real key to his success, as well.

Q. You mentioned earlier with the impact that Coach Bryant had with his players beyond what they were able to do while he was coaching them. How much interaction do you have with your former players, specifically Rolando McClain since he's back on campus?

SABAN: A lot. Specifically with Ro, a lot. I talked a lot to him when he was making the decisions that he made to get back in school, and to come back and work out, as a player who may someday decide he wants to play when he has his mind in the right, you know, sort of to play football.

So quite a bit, you know. We pride ourselves on the fact that our players come back a lot. A lot have been successful. We even have players that have been unsuccessful and suspended and come back and make an impact on our players when they realize that what they did is not the way to go, and they can affect somebody else in a positive way.

I think it's very important. I can't speak for the players themselves, but I always enjoy when the players come back, look for guidance. Most of the players come back for the spring game, A-Day, I think that's always good.

I think most of the guys know that have played for me know if they ever need anything, I'll always be there for them. There's a lot of former players that played for me at LSU that still call and stay in touch.

Q. A few weeks ago you talked about with ESPN about wanting to start over like it was 2007, after the season. I was wondering if you could expound on that, what that exactly means.

SABAN: When you start a program, you focus on the fundamental things that you feel are really important in the program, whether it's everybody buying into the principles and values of the team so that you can be a good team and everybody having a positive attitude about trying to accomplish the goals that you've established for the team, everybody being responsible for their own self-determination that they'll go do the things they need to do so they can do their job well, and the willingness to invest your time and have the discipline to do things at a high level on a consistent basis.

If those are the fundamental things we want to accomplish, sometimes you do inventory and you say we've gotten away from that a little bit and maybe we need to get back to it. So maybe people need to be more accountable to it. Maybe they need to be more aware of it, whether it's coaches, players, myself, whoever is involved.

So that's kind of what I meant by what I said when we got to that, when I made that statement, is we need to get back to the fundamental things that have made us a successful program through the years and everybody has got to trust and believe in those things so that they really know and believe that's what's going to help us be successful.

Q. You knew what you were getting with Lane Kiffin when you hired him. But what is the most important thing he's brought to the team?

SABAN: What I knew I was getting is a very, very good coach, who does a great job with the players, is a great teacher. He is exactly what I thought he was, does what I expected him to do.

He's a really good play caller. He's done a great job for us this year. I think I got exactly what I expected. I don't think anybody else expected what I expected, to the point where I even got criticized for doing it by a lot of people.

But I got what I expected. You all didn't get what you expected. That's what you really want to write about.

Q. We talked to Lane Kiffin yesterday and he gave you some credit for really wanting to bring a more up-tempo, fast-paced type of offense to your team. Can you kind of just talk about that?

SABAN: Well, I think that we try to do the same thing with our team and our players, relative to what we feel would be the most effective thing for them to do so that we can be productive.

And I think that, systematically, for myself or for Lane, neither one of us had really ever been sort of an up-tempo team. But being a defensive guy and knowing the issues and problems that this has created for what we have to face when we play up-tempo teams, for the last season and this season, I've been wanting to move in that direction.

And to Lane's credit, he was very open to trying to implement something that would be effective for our players and certainly did a really, really good job of implementing a system, and some of it was a little bit through trial and error for all of us that helped our players be productive and effective this season.

And I think it worked out very well for the players that we have.

Q. I want to take you back to the end of your first season at Alabama, 2007. What did you maybe have to change or work on to go into the 2008 season that served as a springboard to the success that you've had that year?

SABAN: Boy, I'll tell you what, you know, I think that when you start a program, and I think Dabo probably would agree with all this, because he's done an outstanding job of building a great program at Clemson, is you really have to establish fundamental sort of intangibles that are going to help you build the kind of character, competitive character in the people that you have in the organization to get them to be all that they can be, and that says a lot about the attitude that the players have, and that's certainly a challenge.

To get players to respect and trust in the principles and values, to get players to respect and trust each other, become a family and a team that believes in these things will help us be successful, and having people have sort of a positive attitude and energy about doing those things and being responsible and accountable for their own self-determination in following those things and having the kind of work ethic that it takes to be able to do those things, I think those are the fundamental things that you try to establish. They don't happen overnight. Players have to buy in, and we're very fortunate here in the way the players bought in and the improvements that we were able to make early on.

Q. Talking with a lot of coaches across the country, they talk about your program, great relevance, of course, in terms of them trying to reach the plateau where you're at right now. So often we hear the term gold standard. As the leader of that organization called the University of Alabama football program, talk about the gold standard and what that means to you, what your goals have been as the head coach to reach the highest plateau and to maintain the consistency to stay there over the years.

SABAN: Well, my goal is to create value for our players. That's always been the goal for me as a coach. And I touched on this before in terms of personal development, thoughts, habits, priorities that are going to help guys make good choices and good decisions that will allow them to take advantage of their gifts, which is going to give them a better chance to be successful in their life, how to set a goal, how to understand a process of what you have to do to accomplish a goal, and the discipline it takes to execute that on a day-to-day basis.

Getting an education is a big part of that, so that's something that we really, really emphasize with our players, and we've had success for a number of years being able to do an outstanding job relative to that so that players are developing careers off the field. We want to help them develop as football players. I have a chance to have individual success as a college football player, have team success, have an opportunity to play in games like this or the playoff game that we had last week, and see if they can develop a career as a football player and play at the next level, and we also, being at the University of Alabama, I think, and the tradition that we have and the number of people who associate with the institution, you can also help guys in terms of career development by using the resources that the institution has.

So these are all things that we try to create value for players, which when you have good players and you're able to recruit good players, then you do a good job of creating relationships and helping them develop, I think the end result is you're trying to create value for them and they are doing a good job on the field to try to create value for themselves as football players as well as the program and the team, and that's kind of been what we've tried to do, and that's the standard that we have.

I think the result has been only viewed externally as how many games you win, but that's not really the standard that we operate from internally.

Q. Nick, what will be the next college football focused activity or effort you expect of your players when you get back?

SABAN: Well, I think it's been a long season for our players. I think they need some downtime. We typically, if we play on January 1st, don't start until maybe the last week of January, just the lifting program, a couple weeks of off-season program and a couple weeks after that, try to get them re-centered academically. We start school tomorrow. So that guys get back in the right routine, developing the right habits about what they have to do to be successful in school.

Recruiting is obviously something that we all participate in. It's very important for the players on your team to contribute to recruiting players that they want to play with or can play with in the future who are talented guys that we need to develop relationships with or need to continue to develop relationships with.

So there's a lot of things going on. The bus doesn't stop. You've got to keep rolling and just take things day by day, but I do think that our players need, from a physical standpoint, a little downtime in terms of what they need to do to get ready for next year, because we've had a significant amount of practice that other people wouldn't have at this time of year. So we need to get some guys healthy and get some rest time, get some downtime before we delve into what we want to do for next year.

On if his system is more conducive to having freshmen be able to contribute:

SABAN: I don't know that it is systematic. First of all, the guys that have contributed when they are freshmen are the guys that have shown the maturity to be able to develop as players, and stay with it so that they can become complete players at their position rather than getting frustrated easily about not having immediate success. I think that is one key ingredient to each of those guys. Secondly, it speaks that we have been able to recruit guys that can contribute. I also think that it is a little bit easier to contribute at some positions like wide receiver, running back or maybe even cornerback. If you're an offensive lineman, you need to know who to block on every play, every pass protection and every mistake that you make, someone is going to get blown up. At running back, if you can carry the ball effectively and learn the five or six running plays that you've got, you can do that and you can contribute in the game. You can be a very good receiver and be effective at running certain pass routes and be effective at doing that. You don't have to be complete to contribute at some of those positions, but I think the two guys (T.J. Yeldon and Amari Cooper) that we have that are contributing offensively the most have become pretty complete players quickly. I think that speaks to their maturity, how they practice, what they do every day.

On playing young guys and how much of a luxury that is:

SABAN: I do think that even though they (Florida Atlantic) scored on the last drive, a lot of the guys that got an opportunity to play this week learned a lot about what happened when they played at Arkansas, and that really helped them improve. It improved their preparation. It improved their sense of urgency about getting ready to play, and that they may have an opportunity and they need to be prepared. There was improvement made and I think that's a good thing and I think that helps the depth of our team. On the other side of that, you could say 'we haven't had to play 60 minutes in the game yet with the guys we are going to have to play, and we are going to play against a team that's going to try to run 80 plays on offense, that's their goal.' More players are going to have to contribute and the players that play are going to have to sustain their performance for longer in the game.

On if decisions will start to be made about redshirting freshmen and playing certain freshmen:

We have played a lot of freshmen, and in some cases those guys have developed nicely, and I think they are going to contribute to our team significantly down the road. In other cases, you would like to see guys progress more rapidly, but we are going to continue to work with them and play the guys that we have played. I think if a guy hasn't played to this point, we probably don't plan to play them, but we may not have the luxury to do that. I think that we continue to try to develop all the players that are freshmen and if we get injuries or have an issue or problem with depth at a position, we may have to play someone else who we thought we maybe didn't need to play.

I think again, we are trying to make these decisions based on the fact 'is a guy going to get to play enough to help him develop as a player,' relative to losing the year of eligibility for playing just a little bit and that is really what we are trying to do. We don't have any plans to play anyone to this point that has not played but that doesn't mean that that can't happen or won't happen.

On what makes Alabama different:

SABAN: There is a tremendous tradition here. There is a tremendous amount of passion from the fans that has gone on for many years. All of that is sort of common for the SEC in our league as a whole. I don't really know why that is. Maybe it's because there were not a lot of professional sports in the south east back in the old days and everyone sort of grew up relating to their college team. I think that people do relate to their college teams and their college programs here, whether they went to the school or not more than other parts of the country. I think that is what makes it special here in Alabama but it is also what makes it special in the SEC. When it comes to the rest of it, as a coach, you have to do what you have to do. You have to stay focused on the process of what you need to do in order to be successful. You can't think about all of that stuff. Those are external factors.

The better you can manage not allowing that to affect you so you can focus on what you need to do in order to help your team play the best they can play is probably the most important thing that you can do as a coach. That is what we really try to do. It is difficult sometimes but it is what we need, try, and want to do for our players' sake. I want our players to be able to do that too. I think they can be affected by the passion, the tradition, and all of the external rather than focus on what they need to do in order to be the best players they can be.

On the impact of the Heisman Trophy to the football program:

SABAN: I don't think anybody was thinking about it. I don't think anybody cares about it. I don't think Trent Richardson cares about it. I think if you ask our players, and I don't think about it either, it's about 'what do we have to do to help the team be successful? What do I need to do? What can I do?' Our thoughts are completely different than your thoughts. Completely. So I don't even know how to answer the question, to be honest with you. Trent is a great player. He's one of the best players in the country. Whatever awards they give at the end of the season, he certainly should be considered for any and all of them that he qualifies for, but for right now, we're thinking about what we need to do right now. We're not even concerned about that stuff.

On if the personality of the defense is different than other defenses:

I think there is always a combination when you have a good unit - offense, defense or anything. First of all, you got to have some togetherness. There's got to be some chemistry. I think that we probably have that as a team, but certainly on the individual units on our team and on our defense.

I think there's also got to be a certain amount of physical toughness, sort of a competitive spirit, attitude, whatever, which I think is pretty good with this group. They're all kind of responsible for making sure they do their job. You're only kind of as strong as your weakest link, and I think that they have a lot of pride and everybody wants to go out there and try to do their job the best that they can. I think all the other players expect that as well, and they work hard. They've worked hard, and I think our team has worked hard.

On the identity of the football team:

SABAN: I think you start to establish an identity the first time you play. I think you want to try to build on that identity because that identity can move in one direction or the other, and consistency is what I would be more focused on right now in terms of to continue to play at the level that we play. And the most challenging thing for players is to practice well because the thing that happens is when you don't practice well, you lose fundamentals. You don't play with good fundamentals. That affects your ability to have success in the game.

We play against so many different things that you start getting assignment oriented and thinking of what I'm supposed to do and spend less time practicing and thinking about how I need to do it. And that, to me, is the most important thing as the season progresses so that you improve. I can't tell you what the identity is. You have your own opinion about that. I have my opinion about it. I know some areas that I would like to see it grow and develop, but this team has demonstrated pretty good leadership, and pretty good competitive character to this point, and I'm sure that is going to get challenged on numerous occasions in every game that we play in the future.

What are your policies concerning Twitter?

SABAN: We monitor guys' Twitter. We don't want any guys to put information out there about what happens, but we released the information before the game because we didn't want it to be a distraction to the team. The team knew it, but we didn't want everybody to start focusing on what's happening, and all that kind of stuff. Our team knew what the situation was on Friday. I mean if we'd gotten the information on Saturday morning, the guy could have come up there and played in the game, so we weren't going to make an announcement until we were absolutely certain that wasn't going to happen.

We found that out on Saturday morning, so we thought it would be best to pass out that information during pregame, but our policy is we don't want guys to twitter information about our team that creates an advantage for the other team. And secondly, we monitor guys' Twitter so that they are not putting information out that could be personally damaging to them in the future in terms of the kind of information that they choose to put out there, but we don't have a policy where you can't do it.

On the identity of his team:

SABAN: I really think our team is progressing. Each week you have a new challenge and you learn more about your team. Like how are we going to respond this week? We play another very good team on the road in a difficult place to play. Are we going to be able to challenge ourselves to continue to do the things we need to do to play at a high standard? Are we going to be relieved with what we've done up to this point? I can't answer those questions. They have to come from within, with what people accomplish and what they want to do. So far we've responded fairly well, but not consistently all the time and that is something we have to continue to work on.

On whether having the team full of mostly players he recruited will affect the team's personality:

SABAN: I think the personality of our team has basically come from players buying in, regardless of who brought them in. That has never been an issue. We had a lot of good players last year that we recruited and we brought here, and we had a lot of good players last year that were here when we came here who bought in to the principals and values of the organization and they were more successful because of it. I think who brought them in is insignificant. I think it's what their commitment is and how they buy into the organization, together as a group and individually, that makes the group what it is and what's going to determine the personality of the team and the identity of the team.

On importance of having flexibility to admit special admission students and have there been any success stories:

SABAN: I think we have had a tremendous amount of success

stories, in terms of our graduation rate and the number of players that we've had that have made the Freshman All-SEC Honor Roll because they have over a three-point GPA. I think if you look closely, some of those guys have been special admits, so to speak. So, I am really pleased and happy with the job that we do and how we manage our students here and the responsibility and accountability they have toward academics and the success they have had in academics. But, I also want to reiterate to you my philosophy, I think that, I guess I grew up around land grant schools and land grant schools are supposed to educate all the people and they are not selecting Roman institutions and public schools are not selecting Roman institutions, but they have become that for some reason. So they don't really educate all the people, but we want to create opportunities for people and as long as we feel like they have the character and attitude and will respond to the direction that we give them to have success here and we have a pretty good track record of that with the people that we have, we want to give people an opportunity and we want and we want to give people an opportunity.

It's no different than Terry and I making a significant contribution to first-generation scholarships. We're creating an opportunity for someone who may not have the opportunity if someone didn't help create an opportunity for them. No different than Michel Oher in the movie The Blindside. If somebody didn't help him ... he had the work ethic and the ability to go to college, to graduate and to be a first-round draft pick. Somebody helped him take advantage of his gifts. I think he's better off, the world's better and we all better off because of it. The question I would ask is do we all do enough? Do you do enough? Do I do enough? Do we do enough to help other people take advantage of their gifts. Some people have ability and they have work ethic and really never a get an opportunity.

On the atmosphere at Bryant-Denny Stadium:

SABAN: Well I think I've also spoken about that just about every week. I think our fans have done a tremendous job. I always say our fans are a part of the team, especially last year at the end of the season and the last few games that we've had, the Tennessee game, the South Carolina game, the LSU game. I don't know where you could find a better environment to play a college football game, in terms of the atmosphere created by our fans, the enthusiasm and the passion they have and how it affects the players. I don't think that myself or any of the players don't really appreciate that. I've always said that's important and sometimes it's more important when you're not playing as well, as it is when you're playing really well. We've had both of those circumstances this year and our fans have been very, very positive and supportive in both cases and very helpful in both of those cases. So, we appreciate it. It's important. I'm happy they have the passion. I'm happy they have the enthusiasm, but I also want them to know we appreciate it and it's important to what we're trying to accomplish as well.

On the possibility for a Heisman campaign:

SABAN: I'm not concerned about that. Talk to this guy over here, that's what he gets paid for. Who are you talking about for Mac? I haven't thought about it. I don't think about things like that. I'm kind of worried about playing well in this game. If you play well and you win, those kinds of things seem to take care of themselves. I know in this day and age we are all concerned about how we market things and ourselves, but we're concerned about how we do as a team and I know Mac is as well. I know Greg is. I know everybody in the organization wants to do what we need to do to have success as a team. I don't think there is anything you remember more, I can't tell you how many yards I passed for my senior year in high school, or junior or sophomore.

I can't tell you where we ranked in the Mid-American Conference when we won the MAC Championship when I was a college player. I don't know the statistics. I don't know where we ranked when we won the national championship on offense or defense. I sure do have a pretty good feeling about what the team accomplished. I still remember the sign that says state football champs in my little town in Monongha, West Virginia. It makes me proud when I go to that town.

We are the only team that won the Mid-American at Kent State, ever. That makes me proud. I don't know where we ranked on anything. I don't know who made All-America. I don't know who made All-Conference. I don't know any of that stuff and really if you've got a good team that will be the thing they remember the most. It's like Ronnie Lott said 'you never feel better than when you sell out to the team.'

Saban on today's generation never being told no

SABAN: These guys, they all think they have this illusion of choice like, 'I can do whatever I want to do.' We kind of have a younger generation now that doesn't always get told no. They don't always get told, 'This is exactly how you need to do it.' So they have this illusion they have all these choices. But the fact of the matter is, if you want to be good, you really don't have a lot of choices, because it takes what it takes.

You have to do what you have to do to be successful, so you have to make the choices and decisions to have the discipline and focus to the process of what you need to do to accomplish your goals.

All these guys that think they have a lot of choices are really sadly mistaken. As we all have done with our own children, they learn these lessons of life as they get older. Sometimes, the best way to learn is from the mistakes that you make, even though we all hate to have to see them make them and don't condone it when they do. Geno has done a good job coming back doing what he's supposed to do, and hopefully, he'll finish that up by the end of May and go from there.

Leadership

Q. Players can hear the coaches say focus, focus, focus, but usually it has to come I would think from inside. Can you talk about the role of your quarterback AJ and maybe C.J. defensively and helping that issue?

SABAN: I think that coaches probably can affect things from outside in to some degree, but I think how the team gets affected from inside out probably ultimately determines how much buy-in you really have to whatever any coach says.

Obviously we've had some pretty good leadership on our team from AJ McCarron and C.J. Mosley, both outstanding players. They both love Alabama. It's football is really important to them and how the team does is really important to them.

But I think there's two things about leadership, is you can have great leadership, but there has to be people on the team that is willing to respond to the leadership and to buy in and do the things that they need to do.

And I think that's the critical piece to what is important for our team in this particular game, is everybody going to go dig deep, do the things that they need to do to get back to being the kind of players they're capable of being in terms of how they execute every play in the game for 60minutes in the game.

So that's the challenge. And you can ask me to predict what that's going to be and you can ask me all kind of questions about where we are, but really until we go play, I mean, nobody really knows for sure.

And that's why we play. And so we're going to do everything we can to have our team well prepared mentally and physically to go out and play their best football. How they respond to that sometimes is, you know, not something you can predict.

On the leadership on the team and how important it is for players to be hearing things from other players as well as the coaching staff:

SABAN: I don't think that there is any question about the fact that players probably impact each other more than anyone realizes. It was really interesting. We had a leadership seminar right before the season started. I might not have these questions exactly right, but I think that I can get the point to you. The first question to the players was how important do you feel it is, you personally, that you allow your teammates to know how you feel. Most of the players wrote that they didn't think that they thought it was that important.

We have coaches and other people here that can do that. Next question was, what's the most important thing to you, and the unanimous answer was what my teammates think of what I'm doing. So to me that kind of answers the question that when you have good leadership and you have people that are involved with players, that probably is as significant as anything in terms of a team being able to continue to improve and play with consistency. In the game, I think that those guys can affect the game more than coaches when the game is going on. Someone has to step up and say the right things at the right time. There has to be a conviction and a belief and a faith from the other players that we can do this.

On Julio Jones changing the culture of how wide receivers approach their work at UA:

SABAN: What I was speaking of was not what he does in the game, on the field in terms of his ability to make plays, but it's how he works every day, the toughness that he has, the attitude, preparation and being a hard worker. We're very fortunate here that our best players have been very good people, whether you look at guys from last year whether it's Javier Arenas, Rolando McClain, Kareem Jackson, or whether it's Trent Richardson, Mark Ingram,

Julio, Mark Barron or Dont'a Hightower. Those guys are all really good people. They've got the right stuff character wise and they're very good players. I think that has a tremendous impact on, first of all the other people in your group, but also on your unit. Julio and receivers are sometimes guys who, they should want the ball no doubt, but sometimes can be affected a little when they don't get the ball and don't see other parts of what they do as important to the success of the offense. Julio, because he's such a good blocker, physical and tough, that's sort of permeated throughout the group. I think that's one of reasons we have as many long runs as we do.

On players showing leadership and staying out of trouble:

SABAN: I think we didn't have guys getting in trouble this summer, last summer and for the last year a half because of the individual decisions that they make. I'm not sure that's all about leadership, I think it's about guys understanding what it takes to be successful, and how when they do the wrong things they actually get negative consequences, and when they do the right things they can get positive consequences. Consequences do matter in terms of their chances to be successful as people, as students, as football players and their future development, those things matter.

We've had players here that everybody had high expectations for to get drafted and have great NFL careers that didn't get drafted, and we've had players here that walked on and became third round draft picks. The players see all that, in terms of who did the things they needed to do to create the kind of consequences for themselves that are going to help them be successful. We have a lot of internal programs, the PX2 guys, the Pacific Institute guys had a great summer again with our players and our players enjoy that. We have guys from IMG, Trevor comes in and talks with them.

We do a lot of things to try and develop the right character and attitude - thoughts, habits, and priorities to make good choices and decisions about what you do and what you don't do. We are going to continue to do that. Does that mean that we're never going to have a problem? I doubt it. But, I think we are going to have less because we are going to have the kind of people who are going to make better choices and decisions about what they need to do to be successful, and what their goals are and understand the consequences of not making good decisions.

On the maturity of this team with only nine scholarship seniors:

SABAN: Maturity doesn't always just come with age, but I do think the nine seniors on this team show tremendous leadership. I think some of the younger players on the team have shown a lot of maturity, in the way they've been able to handle the circumstance that they're in. A couple of freshmen have shown a lot of maturity. A couple of sophomore players have shown a lot of maturity. I think it's critical that we stay focused that way as a team and not let other things affect that. As I said before, we are trying to develop a kind of an elite attitude in terms of expectation and what want to try and accomplish. That does not happen overnight. That doesn't happen today, but I think there is a pretty good buy-in with most of the players here, relative to what is expected of them, what they can give and what they are willing to do to help the team try and be successful and I think that is the most important that has contributed to that maturity.

Mindset

Q. You talked earlier about the work of the Pacific Institute. Have you used anything similar to that at any of your other coaching stops? How has that work helped this year's team?

SABAN: Well, we've always done things like that. We have about three or four different people that we've used for years. We have someone from IMG, their mental conditioning, who is with us. We had several people at LSU. We had several people at Michigan State. We have a sports psychiatrist from Michigan who periodically visits and affects our players on an individual basis and has had a significant impact on, you know, helping guys be successful, resonating on things that would help them develop a direction that could help them be successful.

So, you know, I putzed around when I was in graduate school by having a concentration in sports psychology. It was very interesting to me. So this part of - the mental part of the game has always been something that I didn't know enough about, probably knew just enough about to get in trouble, but have always tried to surround our organization or program with some of these people who can impact and have knowledge and experience in that area. And I've seen it over the years have a tremendous impact on performance with a lot of players.

Q. You said you putzed around with psychology and sports psychology. When you read stuff, do you read Freud, Norman Vincent Peel?

SABAN: I'm from West Virginia, man. We don't even know who Freud is up there.

No, I just -- like I read Michael Johnson's book, Slaying the Dragon. I always read Rick Pitino, Pat Riley.

But I spend a lot of time discussing how to manage people with these people who are involved in our program. And I think that it helps you think out of the box a little bit and it gets you out of -- as a coach, you really like the cookie- cutter type of everybody fits the same mold. But I think through the year players have changed dramatically and there's a lot of different personalities that play now. I think your ability to motivate, reach, affect, however you want to say it, these different personalities, but not let their personalities be divisive to the team chemistry, is a key to being successful.

And I can say that a lot of these people that we've had relationships with and work with have certainly helped us expand our thinking and our awareness so that it's helped us do that.

Q. We've talked a lot about the Pacific Institute, the other mental conditioning stuff you've done throughout the season and the summer. How well has that prepared you to handle, not just this week, but also the other situations that have kind of come up around the game?

SABAN: Well, I think part of this is all about self-actualization: who you are, what you want, how you channel your energy in a positive way into accomplishing what you want. I think that's what this is all about. The respect, the trust that you have for each other on a team, the responsibility that everybody has to do the right things, not only for themselves, to help themselves be successful, but also for the team to be successful, the commitment that everybody makes and has a trust and respect for, relative to the work, the pride and performance, the perseverance it takes to overcome adversity.

There's always adversity. There's always circumstances and situations that come up that are challenging for everyone to stay focused on the things that they can control so that they have the best opportunity to be successful. To do all that with positive energy and positive attitude, to affect each other in a positive way, is something that can also be beneficial. That has a lot to do with leadership. I don't think you accomplish what this team accomplished in winning 12 games in a regular season without having a lot of positive leadership on your team.

Q. How often do you find in a game of this nature and this size, a lot of obvious things have been discussed this week, offense, defense, particular marquee players, but at the end of the day, something that was not viewable to us, something that may be able to be viewed decides the game, something very small, something nobody has talked about?

SABAN: Well, you know, that's probably the unknown that keeps you up at night as a coach, like what are we not prepared for, what might happen in the game that if you haven't sort of spent the time to get your players ready to play for, how well will you be able to adjust to those circumstances in the game.

But I really believe that in games like this, the same factors, controlling the line of scrimmage, stopping the run, being able to run the ball, explosive plays, turnovers, red zone efficiency, both sides of the ball, 3rd down efficiency, both sides of the ball; all those same factors that affect outcomes of games probably are going to affect the outcome of this game. And there may be some technical things that happen inside of all that that you weren't prepared for, maybe a formation or whatever it might be, or something that they do on defense, a pressure or a blitz, but your ability to adapt and adjust to that affects your ability to be successful in all those areas that we just talked about. So it's all going to come down to that.

I think in bowl games in general, psychological disposition is really, really important, because I've talked before about how it's so difficult to bring the momentum of the season to this game, regardless of where you were when the season ended, because there's such a separation in the two.

So you've got to kind of look at it as a one-game season, and when you look at these bowl games, you can tell that the way the team approaches it, the passion that they have for it, sometimes is a little bit different, and it does affect the outcome of the game. That's the one challenge as a coach you're always a little concerned about; are you getting that with your players.

On how the Pacific Institute has helped your players:

SABAN: We have a peer-intervention program here, which the Pacific Institute is a part of it and I call their part of it the mental-conditioning part of trying to teach people how to be successful and what it takes to be successful, whether its self-actualization, whether its focus or locking on or locking out. It's all some form of motivation that you try and get people to realize how important it is to be successful. They are one part of that. We usually don't have anyone speak to the team during the season, but we do have a lot of things go on in the summertime and during fall camp. The off-season is probably where we try and make the most significant impact with those people from the outside that we use.

The speaking program that we have has lots of quality speakers that come in and speak about various subjects, whether it is drugs, alcohol, agents, gambling, spiritual development, how to treat the opposite sex, macho man stuff and getting in fights. All the stuff you read about in the paper people suffer consequences for as student-athletes, we try to address in this, in terms of behavioral issues, as well as attitude development both sides and we have a lot of people that contributed to that in a lot of ways.

We are very, very pleased in what the Pacific Institute has brought to the program. Community outreach is also a part of that, so compassion for other people is probably the most important things in terms of qualities that anyone can have and that is certainly something that we want our players to give back to the community and help other people.

On efficiency and attitude of the team the last two weeks and is that the message this week, with the emotion of this game:

SABAN: I think emotion is great. I also think controlled emotion channeling in the right direction and doing the right things. I felt like we have played some games where we got emotional, this game included a couple of years ago, and we make a lot of mental errors and don't execute very well and sort of lose our focus and discipline. I don't think that's the best way to have an efficient performance. I think emotion is great, but it's got to be channeled in the right direction. I think it's important in games like this that the players focus on the things they need to do to be successful and not get caught up in what's going on around them. I do feel that in the last couple of games, we have played a little more consistently, got off to a pretty good start. This is the only game that matters right now that we do a good job that way in this particular game.

On his mindset and attitude heading into fall camp:

SABAN: I think that when you're process oriented and you're driven to try to do things a certain way, and you believe that doing those things that way are going to help you have the best chance for that particular team to be successful, I don't think there is a whole lot of difference.

Every team has a little difference in personality, but at the same time, I think the principles and values that help any team be successful, which are a few of the things I've touched on before, whether it's work ethic, discipline - you know we're talking about the basic will to be successful, how important it is to them, what the determination is, what the commitment is, what the accountability is to the principles and values that everybody buys into. I think those things are the most important to get established. I said this at SEC Media Day, not one player is going to put our team over the top, but one player can destroy our team by not doing what he is supposed to do, by not buying in, by not being responsible to his own self-determination relative to what he needs to do to help our team and help himself be successful.

I don't think those things change a whole lot. I don't think what it takes to be successful changes a whole lot in your life, relative to what's important to you and what you're committed to doing. That part of it stays the same. Every team has needs. There is no perfect team, there is no perfect player. Every player has something that they need to work on to improve. Every player can improve. Every team has issues and problems on their team, relative to personnel, whether it's lack of experience at certain positions or lack of depth at certain positions, and obviously we're going to take every player that we have and do the best we can to put them in the best roster spot so that they can develop to try and satisfy some of those issues on our team so that we can have the best depth that gives us the best opportunity to be consistently successful throughout the season.

Q. Kirby talked yesterday about the mental aspect of the game as it pertains to you coaching now, and he said you're probably more involved with that now than you are the actual defense. Can you talk a little bit about how you get your players to believe in what you say and all the things you do to get their mind right? I know brainwashing is a negative connotation, but in this case is that kind of a good thing?

SABAN: Well, I never thought of what I try to get the players to do as brainwashing, but really what we're trying to do is to get them to be all they can be and try to understand the things that they need to do to do that. And so many times something as simple as running a 40-yard wind sprint, I'll say, we want you to run as fast as you can run, but a guy will run fast enough to beat the guy next to him. So is that really being all you can be, or is that putting sort of a self-imposed limitation on all you can be relative to what the guy is next to you? And that's not really what we're trying to get people to aspire to.

I think really great athletes, whether it's Michael Johnson, Michael Jordan, Mariano Rivera, those guys sort of get it, they understand that the last race doesn't really matter. No matter how many game-winning shots I've made in the past, the only one that really counts is the next one. So what do I need to continue to do to prepare to be able to take advantage of those situations.

I think that's what we're trying to constantly get our players to do, and it's a battle. It's a battle versus human nature, because sometimes they like to get casual in their approach, in their preparation and not do things the way you need to do them to be successful, and that's the challenge that we always have, and we're always looking for ways to inspire them to continue to be all they can be.

Discipline

Q. In light of situations such as Aaron Hernandez's situation, how much responsibility does a head coach have in terms of discipline? How do you make the decision when you have to dismiss a guy like you had to do with four players earlier this year?

SABAN: I think we have a responsibility to create the best atmosphere for the players to have a chance to be successful in, which means that we have to educate our players and the consequences of good and bad behavior, try and create an atmosphere and environment where we're going to get them to have the kind of behaviors that is going to enhance their chances of being successful. I think we have a tremendous responsibility to that.

I think personal development is something that we've always sort of been in the forefront on in terms of human behavior and how we can get people to make choices and decisions that are going to enhance their chances of being successful. So that's something that we've always tried to do a good job in.

We have personal development programs, attitude toward mental conditioning for success. We have peer intervention programs for behavior issues, whether it's drug, alcohol, agents, gambling, how to treat the opposite sex, macho man stuff, getting in fights. We have leadership seminars. We have public relations seminars. Doing everything we can to help our players create value.

But the players have to understand that the consequences of bad behavior is going to be something that affects them as much as anyone. So they have to be responsible to that to some degree.

I mean, any of us that have had adolescents that we've raised, I've had a couple, I know most of you probably have had that experience as well, you know, it's a tremendous responsibility to try to get young people to have the right guidance and inspire them to do the right things. That's something that we've tried to pride ourselves in doing.

I don't think that we're always going to bat a thousand percent when it comes to that. You could be the best professor in the world, be the best teacher, but someone still may cheat on the test. You may provide every single bit of guidance to get the correct behavior, and not, with your own children at times.

So we can be the moral compass for our young people, but we cannot always drive the ship. We always cannot be there to drive the ship. So we're going to try to provide the best moral experience for our players in terms of their development that we possibly can.

You know, I think you have to have a standard of behavior that they understand is the expectation in your organization, and I think they have to understand the consequences if they don't meet that. I don't think there's anything wrong with that.

In the meantime we're going to do everything we can to help them develop that behavior. Human behavior is not an exact science, but we're going to do everything we can to try to help every player have success in his life because he makes good choices and decisions in the program.

On what goes into keeping players out of trouble off the field:

SABAN: Everybody has a responsibility to represent themselves, their family and the institution in a first-class way, and that's what we try to sell to our players. We try to do some educational programs, whether its peer-group intervention or success-oriented-type education that helps players know what's going to help them be successful. I'm sure that every program tries to do that to some degree. I'm sure they've tried to do that at the University of Florida, and I know the people that they have there, the coaches that they have there and what they want and the expectation that they have for the standard for behavior that we're all trying to achieve in college football. We'll continue to do the things that we've always done to try to help our players make good choices and decisions so that they have the best opportunity to try to take advantage of their gifts.

On the purpose of allowing local law enforcement to view practice:

What we try to do with our players is have meetings with the law enforcement officials in this community. We want our players to understand that police provide a great service in our community and it's something that they should respect, understand and know about and develop relationships with. The police are there to help you. I think we've done a good job of that and have a pretty good relationship with those people, and our players do respect that. I think having the guys around some probably helps enhance that a little bit.

Saban on discipline

SABAN: People basically think discipline is punishment. Discipline is actually any kind of punishment that is going to change somebody's behavior. The question you have to ask, just like you would with your own children is, is the guy better off with us with the structure and direction he's going to get and the opportunities he can take advantage of and be somebody other people can emulate with his leadership? Or are we better off throwing him out with the bathwater?

I don't feel like that's always the right thing to do, unless it's really warranted.

That's what our whole country is about. Don't we try to give people opportunities? They obviously have a responsibility to represent and do things a certain way, and we're going to make people accountable to do that and continue to teach them to do that, but at the same time, I don't think discipline is always punishment and punitive action to do what? To make people think, 'Nick Saban's really a tough guy, he kicked this guy off the team'? I'm not sure that's the right way to manage this. We're going to do what's best for the player and our program and our team.

On giving players second chances

SABAN: Where do you want them to be? A guy makes a mistake. Where do you want him to be? You want him to be on the street? Or do you want him to be here graduating?

Muhsin Muhammad, who played 15 years for the Carolina Panthers, played for me at Michigan State. Everybody in the school, every newspaper guy, everybody was killing a guy because he got in trouble, and they said there's no way he should be on our team. I didn't kick him off the team. I suspended him. I made him do some stuff. He graduated from Michigan State, he played 15 years in the league, he's the president of a company now, and he has seven children, and his oldest daughter goes to Princeton.

So who was right? I feel strong about this now, really strong, about all the criticism out there of every guy that's 19 years old that makes a mistake and you all kill them. Some people won't stand up for them. My question to you is, 'Where do you want him to be?' You want to condemn him to a life sentence? Or do you want the guy to have his children going to Princeton?

Chemistry

Q. You've done a good job as has Urban of creating a family atmosphere around your team. Would you talk about how important that is to the development of a team and getting that team concept the way you want it?

SABAN: I think team chemistry is paramount to having success. I think team dynamics are so important to being successful. And I think that everybody sort of being committed to the same goals of what you want to accomplish for your team. And them understanding that those goals are probably going to be the things that actually benefit them the most as well.

That when the team does well, there's more sort of accolades for everybody, more attention for everybody. And also more opportunities for everybody.

But I do think that the things that I talked about before, you know, the respect and the trust, everybody being responsible to do their job, committed to the positive energy and attitude it takes to be a consistent performer and everybody being willing to work and persevere to be the best they can be are all things that are important to team chemistry.

And I think when players understand that, it's clearly defined what's expected of you, this is what's expected of you, and they know everybody has to do those things, I think that contributes to team dynamics in a very positive way as well and that's what we've tried to do. And certainly every indication, Florida's team has done the same thing.

Q. Coaches talk about team chemistry being one of the variables that will turn a good team into a great team. Is team chemistry one of those things that's hard to describe; you just know it when you have it? What can wreck it the quickest?

SABAN: I think team chemistry is important to being successful because it means you have a bunch of players who have a respect for each other and trust in each other. I think that contributes to confidence. I think it contributes to consistency.

I think the whole idea that together everybody can accomplish more is something that we talk about, but the individuals that contribute to that really make the team what it is. Their intensity, their intelligence, how smart they play, the sense of urgency that they have in that particular moment to do what they're supposed to do and respect and trust that everybody will do it is something that contributes to team chemistry.

It takes a lot of positive energy. But I also think when you have a group of guys that have been together and have kind of grown up together, you enhance the chances of having that. But in our circumstance, I think how the young players and the team chemistry sort of forms around the older, and the younger is gonna go a long ways in how successful we can be.

Q. What importance do you put on friendships, personal relationships, between team members? Is that something you and your staff stress to try to maintain cohesiveness? Is that something talked about or something that occurs naturally on good teams?

SABAN: Well, I think that the most important thing comes down to two words: trust and respect, the principles and values of the organization, as well as each other. In other words, your teammates, at least as football players and what they do in the organization, what their role is.

I think every issue that we have between players comes down to one of those two things: trust and respect, or some lack of it, for something or someone. But when you don't have the proper trust and respect for the rules and the principles and values of the organization, it creates a lot of division in your organization and togetherness of your team. Because a guy sitting there saying, Well, this guy didn't do what he was supposed to do, he's not getting penalized, coach didn't penalize him enough, he penalized this guy more.

I think when you have that trust and respect and everybody is responsible to do what they're supposed to do, that creates trust and respect for each other, which is very important to have in team chemistry.

I think we have guys on our team that are very good friends, but I also think we have guys on our team that don't spend a lot of time together off the field, but have a tremendous amount of faith, trust, and confidence, and respect for those people, their character, and what they do as football players. I think that's probably the most important thing.

But we do, I will say this, try to encourage our players to do things together. You know, we have a bowling night in the summer where all the guys go bowling together. So we do give them an opportunity to get to know each other a little bit better outside of football.

Q. At the risk of asking you to brag on your team, what is this team's best quality?

SABAN: Well, to be honest, I think this team has kind of exceeded expectations in terms of-- if you look at all the players that we lost last year, the leadership that we lost, the injuries that we've had, the schedule that we played, the adversity that had to be overcome, the new roles that so many people had on this team, the young players who had opportunities to really kind of show what they could do and how quickly they would mature to be able to do their job in a way that would give us a chance to be successful as a team, I'm really proud of what this team actually was able to accomplish together as a group. The team chemistry, the positive energy that they had, the responsibility that everyone has kind of taken for their own self-determination and sort of doing their job, and the way this team has worked and worked hard together to try to become a very good football team and to try to improve.

And I think it was sort of a joint venture between the coaches, the staff that we have, the attitude that the players had that everybody worked to try to continue to improve, and I think that's why this team is able to create the opportunity they have to play in the National Championship game. That probably is the thing that I'm most impressed with about this team.

Q. Nick, has Blake been the perfect leader for this team? And why have you been so anxious to want to see this team win this game?

SABAN: Well, I think that part of the reason that I love this team so much is we have great team chemistry. We don't have a lot of issues ever. Everybody really sort of supports and helps each other. I think everybody has been all in to the vision of what we want to accomplish this year. And it's really fun to coach guys that have that kind of attitude about what they're trying to accomplish and what they're trying to do.

We have lots of opportunities on our team where guys could be selfish, because we had one receiver that had a fantastic year and maybe they could have caught more balls. Christian Jones is out there blocking like crazy for that guy, and so is De White. Nobody really cares. Everybody really cares about having success and being successful. Everybody kind of has each other's back. In this day and age, the way people are, that's kind of unique, and it's really appreciated by me as a coach to have that kind of group of guys to work with.

9
THE PROCESS

Q. You talked about realistic expectations before. Since you've been hired, Alabama fans are talking national championship. Is it realistic for them to expect you to bring one to Alabama?

SABAN: Well, I think if you just assess, we had a 6 and 7 team last year. You know who's coming back. You know what starters. We're going to win with people and our ability to develop those people to their full potential.

Our success has always been relative to the team of people that we've assembled around us, not necessarily what we've done. I think that's important. I'm talking about players, coaches and everybody who contributes to the success of the program. That's something that we're going to work to build.

What's always been my philosophy is where are we today and what do we need to do today to improve and get better, and our focus is always on improving. The quality of people, the quality of talent, the coaching methodology that we use to try to develop that talent, the togetherness, the people who can help develop that kind of team chemistry that's going to help you be successful.

There's no waving a wand and making all that happen. But we

work hard and go from where we are right now to try to get to where we want to be. There's no real formula for what the timetable to do that is.

But we're going to try to stay focused on the process and not get hung up on the frustration that when you have high expectations and it doesn't happen immediately, how that can affect your performance.

You know, I'm just going to say this to everybody. I talk about it all the time. But, you know, in 1986, a priest gave me a book called The Road Less Traveled. It's a spiritual development. Great book. You ought to read it. Spiritual development, positive attitude book. Priest gives it to me at a banquet. I take it home, I open it up, and the first line in the book says, Life is difficult.

I'm thinking I got a crazy priest here that gave me this book. Give me a positive attitude, spiritual development book, and the first line is a negative statement. But when you read the whole book, it was about if you have -- if you think things are going to be difficult, if you're willing to work and invest your time in something, you think it's going to be hard, then when you do have bumps in the road, all right, you're going to have a more positive attitude about overcoming those things.

If you think everything is going to be easy, then every time something goes wrong you're going to have a tremendous amount of frustration and you're not going to respond to it properly and you're probably not going to be able to continue to improve.

That book, probably as much as anything, developed my philosophy about how to manage and handle expectations. All right? I'm talking about relative to getting the results that you want.

Hey, we want to win. We want our expectations to be to win. All right? But we want to do the things that we need to do to give our players the best opportunity to do that every day as we make progress toward that.

Q. You talked a minute ago about your goal is to get Alabama back to being a dominant program. For the Alabama fans, what's a realistic timetable? What timetable can you give them that's realistic to bring Alabama back to a dominant at national prominent level?

SABAN: We never, ever talk about -- it is what it is. We are where we are. We work every day to try to get it where we want it to be. We're going to make small, incremental improvements to getting there.

You know, obviously the quality of player that we can attract in recruiting, the way we can develop the players that we have, the attitude that we can develop within the organization, I mean, there's so many factors that contribute to that. But I have never as a head coach put a timetable. And every situation is different. You know, sometimes you go into a situation, you have pretty good players in there in disarray. You straighten them out, they start playing pretty good, get confidence, all of a sudden you're pretty good.

You go in other situations where you may not have as many good players, it's going to take a little more time to recruit your way out of it. It's always a combination of all those factors that determine, you know, how soon you can start to be successful.

But we're gonna do everything that we can to continue to build a program that our fans and supporters can be proud of. It's certainly our goal to be one of the teams that's recognized in the SEC as a top, top team again.

Q. I know there were a couple teams with the same proposition, but did your expectations as a team change as the season progressed? As far as the season, was it different than it was say in mid-season, that you might be in this position right now?

SABAN: Well, really what we work hard to do with our players is talk about every game being the most important game that we're playing at that time, and that never really ever changes. We try not to allow expectations to affect how they prepare or what their competitive attitude really is about playing in the game.

It's a little bit like Tiger Woods said; somebody asked him how do you manage handling all the pressure that goes with trying to make a putt that's going to give you an opportunity to get in a playoff in the U.S. Open, and he said, well, when you're in the moment, it's really nothing like being a fan because you're focusing on the things you need to do to make the putt. You're not really thinking about the consequences of whether you make it or you don't make it. And as a competitor that's how we try to keep our players focused on the things they need to do to play well, their identity as a team, what helps them play winning football.

And regardless of the game, they're all important. I don't think how we could define which game this year was important. We had lots of important games, and this is obviously one of those games.

I think the best opportunity we're going to have to be successful in the game is be who we are, compete the way we compete, play the way we need to play, and that will give us the opportunity to be successful, and that's what we want our players to focus on.

Q. When you have a new coach come in and take over a program, he talks about a five-year plan. You're in the second year. Have you exceeded your expectations when you came in, what you guys have been able to accomplish?

SABAN: Right. Well, first of all, I don't have any expectations. I get asked those questions all the time. You know, we have goals and we have things that we work towards. We have a process that we put in place systematically, whether it's recruiting, player development, installing systems and keeping them well and finding out what roles the person you have can play effectively and efficiently for you so you get your execution where you can play good football.

You do that day-to-day, and that's the way we've done it, and I've never said we have a five-year plan anyplace I've ever been. I always just say we're going to do everything we can do 365 days a year, one day at a time, to try to improve our organization and make our team better. Some of that is recruiting, some of it is player development, some of it is teaching. But we try to put as many facets together in the program to help the players have success as people, as students and as football players, so they have a better opportunity to be successful in life.

Normally when you build that, everybody starts playing at a little bit higher level and you buy in and see tremendous improvement.

Q. Just a follow-up question on the process, and the question really about freshmen and freshmen playing, in particular Julio Jones. I believe you have a rule that freshmen are off-limits to the media as far as interviews. If you can, just give us a comment or two about Julio and maybe Dont'a's play and how protecting them from the media allows them to mature and give a better performance on the field?

SABAN: Well, I don't have the answer to that question. I know that everybody in this room thinks they should be available and it would help them play better. I don't know that that's true, either. And I don't know that my way is true. I just know that there is a reason for what we do, and it comes from experience of once allowing young players to talk to the media and having them embarrass themselves because of their lack of maturity to be able to handle circumstances and situations before they were able to prepare themselves to be able to do it.

I apologize for that. It's certainly not trying to keep anything away from anybody, and there will be a time when we allow these players to be available to the media.

But just so you know, they're not coming and beating on the door saying, Coach, when do I get to talk to the press. But both guys have done an outstanding job. They've shown tremendous maturity for their age in terms of their development, and I think the players around them have been very supportive in engaging them into the team and helping support them in a positive way so it has enhanced their development.

I think one of the most difficult things for young players is they have expectations because they're five stars and this and that, and then they come into a new venue as a college football player and sometimes don't remember the things they need to do to be productive, good players, and they start all over and they get frustrated when they don't have immediate self-gratification by playing time or having success or whatever, and that actually inhibits their performance because they can't stay focused on the things they need to do to become good players.

In these two guys' case, they and also Mark Ingram, those three freshmen have all shown an ability to do that with the help and support of the players around them, and they've all contributed significantly in the success of the team.

Q. I don't know if the right word is a sense of relief, but the goal was to get to this game. Is there a greater sense of accomplishment? Is it relieve that it's here now?

SABAN: The goal is to be a champion. And I didn't say win a championship. I said be a champion. That's our goal here. That's what we want to do. We want the kind of togetherness, respect and trust that we need on our team to be a team, where everybody plays together and understands that importance of positive energy and attitude in trying to be a good team, everybody being responsible for their own self-determination and doing their job.

Everybody working hard and committed to doing the things they need to do to be the best they can be and that's what we continue to try to strive for and that's what we strive for every week with our team.

And there's really no sense of relief -- there's no complacency. There's no place for that, to me, in competitive sports, because until you win the last -- until you finish the last play of the last game, there's still another challenge out there. And we certainly have a great challenge this week and we're certainly looking forward to the opportunity that that challenge presents to us.

Q. Coach, the cliché is that when you get to this game and don't win it, you immediately start working to get back to win it. How much truth is there in that and how much did you put into, A, getting back to this game, and, B, in particular, that we're going to face this opponent, how much work did you put into them over the offseason and at other times?

SABAN: I think there was a time when we had a team meeting after the Sugar Bowl right before we started the offseason program back in February that we kind of showed a picture to the players of the SEC Championship, and we also said that there were some great teams and we would have some difficult times, but that we had to work to beat the best team in our league. And right now the best team in our league is a team that beat us in the SEC Championship game.

And everything you do, every time you go to work, every time we lift weights, every time you run, every time we practice, it's not to be as good as the guy you're playing against, it's to be as good as the guy you have to beat to be the champion.

And that's the best team in the league. And our players bought into that. They worked extremely hard. I'd also like to say that this team, different than last year's team, had to have that kind of attitude because of expectations. A lot of people had a lot of expectations based on last year. Last year's team wanted to prove they could be a good team.

This team wanted to prove that they could do something special and they wanted to be as good as they could possibly be. And that's how they worked. And that was the buy-in. And I think that's why playing in this game last year indirectly was a lesson that we all learned.

I think we also learned that when you play in championship games, you can pretty much assume that the other team's going to be pretty good, and you can pretty much assume that they're going to have resolve and they're going to want to win the game. And it's going to take an undying relentless, not to be denied attitude to be able to be a champion. I think that's what we learned last year. That's how we played this game. And that's how we won the game as a team.

On not being satisfied

SABAN: We're in the entertainment business. In some of these -- there are other elements that are out there that can affect people's ability to perform. I mean, even guys that get national awards or make All-American, is that the finish line or is that the starting point of what they can accomplish in their future?

I told our players a story the other day about the U.S. Hockey team. Probably one of the greatest victories of this century by any team was when they beat the Soviets in '80 or whenever it was, the Miracle on Ice. Do you know what people don't remember? That didn't win the gold medal; they had to win the next game against Finland to win the gold medal. So what did they learn when they beat the Soviets? They learned when they made a commitment and everybody had a single-minded purpose and I-won't-be-denied kind of attitude and everybody went out there and played their best what they could accomplish. And then they had to go play another game.

And hopefully they learned that and built on that. I think they all built on that because there was a lot of people on that team that had a lot of success and they did win the game, so they did learn something from it.

Hopefully our players will learn some of the same things from what they did in the SEC Championship game and be able to stay focused on those things, because if we don't then you let in all the outside influences.

The first thing I did when we came back from the SEC Championship game in the first meeting is I drew a line on the grease board all the way across the room, the team meeting room, and I said it's 32 days until we play the game; here's the SEC Championship, here's the National Championship. How you manage those 32 days is going to determine how you play in the game. And I can't control that for everybody in this room; you have to make those choices and decisions for yourself. And I mentioned all the things, how you condition yourself; what your weight, discipline is; choices and decisions you make off the field; how you're going to manage agents, media. Guys are going to get recognized and get accolades for accomplishments. Is that going to affect your ability? Is that going to be the final destination for you, or is that just a starting point for what you can accomplish in the future by being recognized for what you accomplished in the past?

So all those things are factors in how we play in a game. And that's what I call clutter, because when you're thinking about that you you're not thinking about what you need to do to prepare to play your best in the game. I know everybody thinks I'm crazy, but that's the way it is.

Q. You talk a lot about pride, discipline, commitment, toughness and effort. How do you settle on those concepts, and when and why did you settle on those as the backbone of your program?

SABAN: Well, I think that intangibles are probably really important to being a good competitor, and I think that most people who have passion for something as important to them is what gets them to commit to something, and your mind kind of does whatever you tell it to do. So once you have the passion and the commitment, at least you're going to be moving in the right direction when it comes to work ethic, discipline, trying to make good choices and decisions about what you do and what you don't do.

The effort, the toughness and the discipline to execute are probably the key ingredients in any sport -- and when I say toughness, I'm talking about mental probably as much as physical, so that you can sustain and overcome adversity and persevere tough circumstances.

I think those are sort of part of your character and who you are, and I think the same ingredients would be necessary to be successful in anything.

Q. If each season and each team is its own separate entity, you were public about saying it wasn't this year's group that won a national title, it was last year's title. Do you think this group understands what that meant?

SABAN: I think they understood right from the start. There's quite a few guys on this team that were on the 2010 team that probably didn't live up to expectations after having success in 2009. I think at least to have some leadership and some experience in the group that saw the difference between the 2010 and 2011 team in terms of just the whole approach, the whole sort of competitive character, attitude, being hungry, whatever you want to call it, I think they realized that the legacy of this team would be defined by what they did and what last year's team did wouldn't have anything to do with that.

I've been pretty pleased with the way this team has tried to respond to it. They've put themselves in a position to have a chance to play in the SEC Championship game, which is a very positive step.

Q. When you talk about the process, what does that mean?

SABAN: Well, the process is really what you have to do day in and day out to be successful. We try to define the standard that we want everybody to sort of work toward, adhere to, and do it on a consistent basis. And the things that I talked about before, being responsible for your own self-determination, having a positive attitude, having great work ethic, having discipline to be able to execute on a consistent basis, whatever it is you're choosing to do, those are the things that we try to focus on, and we don't try to focus as much on outcomes as we do on being all that you can be and the things that you need to do to be all you can be. Eliminate the clutter and all the things that are going on outside, and focus on the things that you can control with how you sort of go about and take care of your business. That's something that's ongoing, and it can never change.

So it's the process of what it takes to be successful, very simply.

Q. I have two parts: One, you said this team exceeded expectations, what were your expectations? And two, everyone talks about talent. Besides talent, what is important for a team to have to get to this stage and win on this stage?

SABAN: Well, I think that the most important thing is how do you approach the game. What's your passion, what's your understanding of the situation that you're in, what's your ability, because you understand the opportunity that you have and the magnitude of that opportunity and how long-lasting the effect and outcome of that opportunity can be. How can you stay focused on the things that are going to help you execute and be successful?

We just watched a video of Mariano Rivera, and he talked about he struggled at some time in his career because he was trying to be a perfectionist, and that when he's in the bullpen, he sees the crowd, he hears the crowd, he knows sometimes that he's being-- getting a lot of positive self-gratification for what he does and sometimes getting a lot of negative self-gratification for what he does. But when he runs out and they hand him the ball, he's got one focus; he's not worried about the crowd, he's not worried about any of the external factors. One focus: Three outs; how am I going to get three outs.

I think a team's ability to do that, to stay focused on the things that are going to affect the outcome of the game, are critical in games like this. And you know, you could say, well, that's nothing; well, believe me, being around young people, being in games like this, that's something, and it's something big. And it certainly affects your ability to perform. The way you'd like to perform and you want to perform is your ability to stay focused on the present-moment things that will affect your performance and to stay in the right sort of disposition that way.

You know, expectations for a team, I never really ever sit down and say, okay, I expect this team to win this many games or this many games or whatever. I just knew there were a lot of challenges for this team in terms of the players that we lost, the things that needed to be overcome, certainly sort of what you're always trying to overcome, which is I call it the entitlement factor when you have success. Are people going to buy in, work hard, do the things they need to do, or are they going to say, why are we doing this? Are they going to work the way you need them to work, because it's human nature that when you have success, you're supposed to get a couple days off, right? When I meet my quota for the month, I'm going to South Beach, right? I mean, that's human nature. That's what we all sort of kind of grow up to be, because we're trying to survive, and survival is what's the self-imposed limitation on what you expect to accomplish.

So that was the challenge for this team, to be able not to have that, not to do that, to take what they could do as a team and really work on developing that in a positive way. So I think that's probably the thing I'm most proud of.

And now it's about can you finish that? Can you finish that? We have 24 more hours as a team; can you finish that?

Q. You talked about this being a building year for the team. Was there talk of an SEC or national championship from the beginning? If so, how did the players react after the Ole Miss loss?

SABAN: Well, we never, ever really talk about that, to be honest with you. We have never talked about it in any year whether we've had the opportunity to win one, get in one, play in the SEC Championship game.

I think our focus is really about taking our team from wherever it is and trying to improve them so that they can be the best team they can be. That was certainly the approach that we took with this year's team.

Ultimately our players have high expectations for what they want to accomplish. They set their goals for what they want to accomplish as a team. In those goals have never been winning the SEC and have never been winning a national championship for any of our teams.

It is a lot about being the best that you can be, trying to do the things you need to do to dominate the competition, to dominate your box, to be the best player that you can be on the most consistent basis, to overcome adversity and compete well for 60 minutes in the game, play together as a team, trust in each other, affect other people in a positive way.

Those are more the types of things I think we try to emphasize with our teams so that we have the opportunity to sort of grow and develop and be all we can be.

Q. Being the new system with the playoff, having to be asked every week about the playoff, did it get old?

SABAN: Personally, our staff, doesn't really look at the rankings of week-in and week-out, because I think we all realize that it's not where you are right now; it's where you end up that's most important.

So you have to keep focusing on the next game and try to do the best you can to get your players to be well prepared and to play their best and continue to improve throughout the season; so that you end up in the right place.

I think the challenge is to get the players and the people in your organization, your staff and everyone to, you know, realize that, sell that, and stay focused on the things that are going to affect their performance and not get sort of affected by the external factors like a poll, like a ranking, like a scoreboard. All those things sort of can change how you compete and how you play.

So I'm not speaking for everybody else, but to me, it's just another distraction that you have to sort of overcome with your players to stay focused on what they need to do to play well.

Q. You mentioned that what you've been able to do at Alabama. How much pride do you take in that in a time when college football is increasingly competitive, that your program has been able to stay up at the top and set the standard for the rest of the country?

SABAN: Well, I think there's a lot of good programs in the country, and a lot of people have had a lot of success. And we have a so-called vision of what we want to accomplish, and we have a process that we think is effective when people buy into it, and we try to create the discipline for the people involved to be able to execute that sort of process.

And I think that's been the key to our success. I also think that from a program standpoint and from a total administrative standpoint, from a university standpoint as well as from an athletic department standpoint, we've been able to create a program that provides a lot of value for players in terms of how we try to use this process to help them be more successful in life for some of the things that they learn in the program.

The importance of getting an education, developing a career off the field, doing the things that you need to do to develop as a football player so that you may have a career as a football player someday if that's your goals and aspirations but always keeping being a good person, developing a career off the field and developing a career on the field, relative to the importance of how is that going to help you be successful in your future.

And that's something that I'm very thankful that our institution has done everything they can to help our players have the best chance to be successful long term in their life.

And it's very-- there's a lot of self-gratification in seeing that happen for young people developing the kind of characteristics that will help them be successful on and off the field.

On the 24-hour victory rule this week:

SABAN: I think that is up to every player making a choice. I think that there are some obvious examples in this game that when you don't do the right things, when you don't pay attention to detail, there are going to be consequences for it. I think regardless of the outcome, players need to understand the importance of paying attention to detail and doing the little things right so that we can get those things fixed and we have to forget about this last game. We have to move on - I told the players that right after the game and I think they have a lot of respect for this team. It would be pretty difficult not to respect this team based on their body of work and what they have accomplished this season.

On if AJ is affected by the attention caused by Heisman trophy talk:

SABAN: I think that the most important thing that we try to get our players to understand, AJ included, is that the most important thing is how you play and how you execute. It is one play at a time, every play in the game like it has a history and life of its own. We are all for our guys getting recognition and we are pleased and flattered that some of our players are up for awards and have a chance to be recognized for their hard work and effort. At the same time I think that they all need to understand that you have never really arrived in terms of what has happened in the past. You are only trying to build on it so you can improve in the future.

To keep your head in the right place relative to your preparation and what it takes for you to go out and play well. Everyone knows what that recipe is for them. It's just like when your mother makes a good cake. As long as she uses the same ingredients, I love that carrot cake, but if she changes the ingredients the cake won't taste the same. It's the same thing with players. I think that is important regardless of whatever external factors are out there, you need to focus on what you need to do to play well in the game. That is what we have tried to emphasize to all of our players. We don't want them to get affected by what other people are saying because the most important thing is continuing to play well. Same thing with players that could be high draft picks. At the end of the day, the most important thing is how did I play so what do you need to do in order to do that.

On sustaining coaching success throughout the years:

SABAN: We are process-oriented in what we do. We are trying to make this team as good as we can make this team. You lose 25 percent of your team every year in college football; you have a whole different team, a whole different mindset, different chemistry, character, strengths and weaknesses, things that you have to do to work hard to try to get young players to have the maturity that they need to have to go out there and play winning football. That's what we are focusing on, and we are not thinking about some result. We are thinking about the game we have this week, and what this game will tell us about our team that's going to help us improve for the next week. That's how you approach the season as a coach, and that's what we are focused on trying to do.

On the standard and knowing if the guys are playing to it:

SABAN: Who you are is who you are every day. How do you practice? How do you decide to do things? What choices do you make about how you do things? How important is it for you to do things the right way? And that all carries over into how you're going to play in the game on Saturday so all these things are important. Everybody needs to focus, be accountable and be responsible for doing the things that they need to do to improve. I've been saying this every week, all year. This is not new, it's not a new message. It just happens to be after we lost everybody is willing to listen because you all are like everybody else, like the fans, 'Oh he's just saying that because he's the coach. They're doing everything they're supposed to do. They won.'

That doesn't mean that you're doing what you're supposed to do. That doesn't mean you're playing the best you can play. What did I say last week? At this time of the year if you're not doing things right you're going to get exposed. Well, we had some guys who got exposed, whether it's the left tackle, whether it's the right corner. What are you going to do about it? That's the question.

On your Friday night routine:

SABAN: We only go to a movie if we have a night game. If we have a night game, we go to a movie. We usually have about an hour long meeting on Friday night. If we have a night game on Saturday, we transfer about two-thirds of that meeting to Saturday after breakfast. So we take a walk on Saturday, have a meeting and sort of get the guys re-centered on the game. So we go to a movie on Friday night if we have a night game. That's been pretty consistent. I usually consult with the players as to what movie they want to see and sometimes we go to see current movies and sometimes we go see old favorites, inspirational-type movies that in some cases the players haven't had the opportunity to see in the past. We didn't have a lot of choices in Starkville, so we did the best we could.

On how you teach your team to stay focused from week to week:

SABAN: I think it's a lot of things and I talk about them every week. So, at the risk of being redundant, it's about who you are. It's about you wanting to be the best you can be. It's about you constantly trying to be responsible for your own self-determination and do your job, the job you're being depended on to do, and do it for yourself and for your teammates. It's also about doing it in any circumstance and any situation, regardless of what's happening around you and who you're playing really doesn't matter as much what you do and how you do it.

The last thing is having the perseverance to be able to do it week in and week out, down in and down out and play in and play out, and those are all the kinds of things you want to condition you're guys to do. You've got to have mental toughness to do it. You have to have the willingness on the part of the players to give the effort to do it and you have to have the work ethic to do it and also the mental intensity to focus on what they have to do to be able to execute it and do their job. It's a combination of all those things I think. We control who we are. That's what we can control and that's what I want our players to focus on being able to do and we talk about that all the time.

On how well this year's team has bought into the one-game-at-a-time approach:

SABAN: So far, so good. The challenge is the next game and how are you going to respond to the next game. I think it gets more and more difficult to maintain that level of consistency, mentally, because each and every team that we play is capable of beating any team on any given day. This team is right down to the wire with LSU, had it first and one at the one or two, or whatever, and didn't punch it in to win. But yet, LSU is the game of the year and this game is like … I don't see it that way and I don't want the players to see it that way. That's a perception that's created by, and I would not accuse anybody in this room of creating anything of the kind, so I don't want anybody to really think that; but in some kind of way it gets perceived and that's what we call clutter.

On if your message to the players changes the last four games of the season:

SABAN: No. I think we focus on the same things all the time, in terms of what it takes to play winning football. That's what you want the players to focus on. I know it's a result world, but great competitors don't focus on the results they focus on what they need to do to get the results. Sometimes that's difficult to do with a lot of the external things that we live with, but that's the most important thing to playing you're best. Maybe we were affected by that a little bit in the last couple of games. I takes away you're aggressiveness. I've said it before, you want to be aggressive and have high-achievement motivation in what you're doing, not lots of anxiety. Low anxiety, high-achievement motivation is the best way to get results. That's what we're always trying to promote and the best way to do that is to focus on the things you need to do to have success.

Starting with such a big game, how does it work with confidence if you win or should you guys happen to lose?

SABAN: I think that the big thing is who you are, what I said before: finding about yourself in terms of how you compete, how you play, who the leaders are. So it's really more about our team and winning or losing really doesn't determine that. How the guys play on individual plays, how they compete, how they can refocus. Can you go out there and give five seconds and do it multiple times and not be affected when you don't have success? Be able to deal with success when you so that your consistency and performance and your ability to finish is better.

This is one game in the season. The way I figure it, you can win and go 1-11. You can lose and go 11-1. And I know that doesn't make good media coverage, but that's the fact of the matter. Obviously we want to win. I think our players want to win. That's what we work hard for. That's what we're preparing for. It's really more about finding out who we are and where we've got to go to get to where we want to be.

Q. Nick, have you guys played your best game yet? If not, is that a reassuring feeling going into the playoff?

SABAN: Well, I always think that we can improve. We certainly didn't play as well today, but I think there was a little confusion because of some of the things that they did that we hadn't practiced. Our guys usually do a really good job of whatever we prepare for, they do a really good job of executing on the field, and they're really good at adjusting to things during the game. But when we see things that are a little bit different, sometimes it creates a little confusion, and I think that was the issue today.

We didn't start the game very well offensively although we finished the game well. I think, if we can create balance offensively and be a little more efficient and effective to how we pass the ball relative to how we can run it, I think that would make us better. So there's a lot of things I think we can improve on. Red zone. I thought special teams was a little better today. That was something I was a little concerned about after the Auburn game. Ball security was not good in that game. It was very good today. We won the turnover battle by three. So we had the three interceptions, and we always say that we want every drive to end in a kick, and that's certainly what happened today.

Q. How hard is it to go undefeated and why should these two teams be-- the won/loss right now?

SABAN: Well, I think it's very difficult in this day and age, especially when you play in a league of our caliber, where we have six teams in the Top-10 I think. I don't look at that stuff quite often but I know there's a lot of good teams in our league.

I think that the consistency in performance is what defines success and I think that's the most difficult thing to get any team to do, especially guys that are student athletes at the college level to be able to focus and play to a standard week-in and week-out I think is one of the most challenging things that any coach, or specifically we have to try to deal with, to get our guys to prepare for the game, focus on the right things. There's a lot of attention out there relative to just who gets in the National Championship game.

So there's a lot of external factors, a lot of external clutter that can affect young people and their ability to focus and continue to do the things they need to do to play at the highest standard. Those are all challenges that we have to deal with to get our teams to play with consistency.

So I think that if you don't have a lot of big games and you don't play a lot of teams that if you don't play well, you're not going to have a chance to be successful, which is just about every team that we played in our division, if we didn't play well, we may not have a chance to be successful. They had enough good players and enough talented people that they could beat us so, that consistency in performance becomes very, very important. There's no time to just, you know, sort of play a bad game and still have a chance to be successful.

So I think that's one of the difficulties of going undefeated. I think that you see it in players late in the season. I saw it in our players when we played Texas A&M that their personality sort of changes from a competitive standpoint and maybe it's feeling the pressure, I don't know. I saw it a little bit in some of the games that I watched with some other highly-ranked teams.

But when you become outcome-oriented, you get tentative, and you're not aggressive play-in and play-out. I think the most challenging thing we have to do to continue to play with success is focus on what's happening right now; and know that when you run for a Gold Medal, you're not really running for the Gold Medal. You're running to run a 19:30, 200-meter race with Michael Johnson or whoever it might be.

So that's got to be the focus, run a good race; play a good game. It can't be what's going to happen if we don't. It's got to be, what do I need to do to do that.

On using a formula from the 2003 BCS Game to help you in this game with Texas:

SABAN: I guess it's like all the other formulas. If it works, it's a good one and if it doesn't you sort of look back on it and try to re-analyze it. But really in all these bowl games, not just this game, it's usually a long time and through the years we feel like we've improved our ability to manage this kind of time and how we practice and how we break down the practices and how many practices you need to have. I think sometimes it's worked extremely well. We didn't practice a whole lot different for the national championship game in

2003 that we did last year for the Utah game. In one circumstance it worked pretty good and the other circumstance it didn't, but I think there are a lot of other factors that contribute to that. We have a theory that if you practice all the time over that period of time, it's going to be very difficult for the players. You need to approach it like it's a one-game season. Let them work out on their own a little bit. Let them work out while they are here in school and then when your start practicing really try and get them into it like you're starting over, which you're not, but that two weeks or so that you didn't have that much practice you let them work back into where they need to be and hopefully you will peak at the right time.

On the factors that have changed the environment of the Alabama program and has it happened faster than you thought:

SABAN: I didn't have any expectations of how fast it would happen. I've said many times before and I say it to myself many times every day, one thing at a time. Solve one problem at a time, whether it's in the game plan, kicking game plan, whatever it is. Whether it's recruiting or personnel and just keep focusing on trying to get better in what you do and trying to get everybody in the organization better at what they do. I think a lot of things that change the program are character and attitude and the way people are responsible and accountable to do their job.

That takes a certain amount of discipline, work ethic, perseverance, ability to overcome adversity, stay tuned to the task and a lot of pride in performance to be the best you can be. I think that each year we've made progress in that regard and we win because we have good players that have good attitudes and work hard and are good at what they do. A lot of the players that have been here have improved as players and we've recruited some pretty good players that have improved as players as well. I think it's a combination of all those things that has helped us get better and make improvement over that three-year time period that you talked about.

On the importance of winning, but in terms of rankings winning a 'beauty contest':

SABAN: We don't focus on that. We are just trying to get our team to play as well as they can play. We are not concerned about that and we're not concerned about the rankings or ratings. We want our team to play the best football they can play. We'd like to get our players, individually, to play to their capacity, as well as our team to play with consistency and to their capacity and focus on improving and consistency. I think those are things we can control and those are the things we focus on and want to try to do. Those external factors are created for fans, which is great, and for the media, which is great, and it creates a lot of interest in our game.

But, as competitors, we have to focus on what we are doing and do it well. There is a lot of good competition out there and so for everybody to continue to improve, so that we can get better are the things we need to be focusing on.

On grading the offense, defense and special teams and where the areas for improvement are:

SABAN: Well I don't really grade them, I just focus on things that we need to do better. I think the biggest thing that we've had to work on is dealing with some of the players that we've lost, especially on special teams. That has really sort of affected the continuity that we have on special teams. We've had to move guys around and shift, and you really kind of lose the cumulative effect of the experience that you gain from week to week to week when you have to do that.

That's something that we're working hard on to get those players enough knowledge and experience to be able to go out there and execute and do well at those positions. That's one of the challenging things that we have to do. I just think on offense and defense we have to play with more consistency, play at a high level all the time, play to a standard all the time, which is what I continue to harp about, so that we're going to give ourselves the best opportunity to be successful.

If you liked this book, you'll love
THE BIG BOOK OF BELICHICK
HIS THOUGHTS ON STRATEGY, HISTORY, AND
FUNDAMENTALS

*Take a look at some selected passages from the book, and
then go to AlexKirbyFootball.com to get your copy!*

Q: It looked like the Giants tried to run a couple rub routes on
their final drive. How do your cornerbacks work in tandem to
defend those routes? Is it coordinated pre-play or is it based on
something they see as the play unfolds?

BB: Right, any time you're in man-to-man coverage and there is
multiple people involved – two-on-two, three-on-three or sometimes
you can be three-on two or four-on-three, whatever it happens to be
– yeah, I think the communication is the key thing there. There are a
lot of different ways you can play it. The most important thing is that

you clearly know how you're playing it and everybody is playing it the same way. If one guy is playing it one way and the other guy is playing it another way, then you're dead. Yeah, so on two-on-two's, we can combo those and switch them.

Sometimes the rule changes a little bit about when we switch or when we don't depending on the type of route that they run. Yeah, that was the case. I think on the first play, which was a second-down play, we also got some pressure on that play with I want to say it was Akiem Hicks and maybe Rob Ninkovich coming off the edge there. I don't know if it would have got to Eli Manning because he kind of grabbed it and threw it but there wasn't a lot of time for him to sort out the pattern, whereas on the second one it was kind of a rollout play and then that extended a little bit longer all the way to the sideline and finally whoever it was – Rob or Malcolm Butler or somebody – came up there and kind of forced him to …

He just went down and took the sack and kept the clock running. But the first play he really never got outside at all. It was just pressure and Logan Ryan took the outside route to Dwayne Harris and then Malcolm kind of fell off it and the combination of the pressure and the coverage, there just wasn't much there.

Q: When a guy moves from the outside to the inside, what are the adjustments they need to make? I know you're supposed to play with good leverage all the time, but is playing with good leverage the most important adjustment you have to make when moving inside?

BB: Yeah, I think you put it well. You always want to play with good leverage, no matter where you are, but the players out at the end of the line – the tackles and the defensive ends are generally longer and maybe have a little tendency to play higher. A lot of times you have players that are a little bit shorter in there in the interior positions, although there are some six-foot-four guards, too, so I wouldn't characterize them all that way. But generally speaking, there's a little less length inside than outside. I think the biggest difference, though, is just how fast everything happens inside and how quickly they have to react, whichever side of the ball they're on. I don't know what the percentage is, but it's got to be pretty high – 85 percent, 90 percent of the time, the offensive tackle blocks the defensive end, in a four-man line anyway.

If you did that on every play offensively, you'd probably get most of them right. Inside, it's a little bit different. Centers and guards block combinations of linebackers and defensive linemen, depending on how the plays unfold and if there is movement inside, which usually there is a little more movement inside than there is outside. For a defensive tackle, you have the potential down-block, double team blocks from both sides – both the tackle and guard, center and guard, or if you're on the nose, from either guard with the center.

So, it's a lot of more of a question of where they're coming from, whereas for a defensive end, the number of times he gets down-blocked by a tight end, it happens, but the frequency is a lot lower. How quickly those guys are on you and how they can come from different spots, it's a much higher variety and it happens pretty quickly. I'd say that's the big adjustment in there.

Q: Do you have a go-to list of how you want to approach game-day coaching?

BB: I definitely believe in a process. I don't know that that's the same in every single game. Well, I'd say it's not the same in every single game. It depends on who you're playing and kind of what they do or what you anticipate them doing as to how you want to approach it. It's a great question. It's a very interesting point of discussion. I think there are a lot of things to look at throughout that, but it's all critical in the communication and coordination of processing the information that you get during the game, I'd say it's not easy to do. I'm not saying it's impossible, but it's not easy to do because it comes from a lot of different sources and you definitely want to prioritize it. I'd say those are some of the components of it.

Number one, getting the most important things handled – whatever they are. It could be what you're doing, it could be what they're doing, it could be the weather conditions – whatever the most important things are making sure that you start at the top. And also you don't have all day. You don't even know how long you have. If you're on defense the offense could be out there for a seven-minute drive, they could be out there for a 30-second drive, so you've got to prioritize what you're doing so that you get to the most important things first, so if you're running out of time, you haven't used your time inefficiently. So that's number one.

Number two, there's the, what we're doing versus what they're doing. A lot of times just making sure that you're right is more important than identifying what they're doing. Sometimes identifying what they're doing, until you get that cleared up then you're kind of spinning your wheels in the sand and you're not making any progress because you don't really understand exactly what the issues are. In the game situation that changes all that. You have the information from players, which is they're in the heat of the battle. You have information from the press box, who can get as much of an overview as you can get. You have sideline information. So sometimes that's the same, sometimes information – you don't see it quite the same way.

The way one coach sees it, the way the press box sees it, the way the sideline sees it, the way a player on the field sees it, it's not quite all the same way. So you've kind of got to sort all that out. And then there is the balance of fixing what is in the rearview mirror and looking ahead. So like, OK we've got to take care of these problems, here's what happened, but at the same time, you're spending all your time on that, some of that is not even relevant because the next time you go out there, OK what are we going to do? We've corrected those problems, maybe we're going to make a different call or maybe we're going to be in a different situation, how do we handle that? So there is the balancing of new information versus analysis of previous information.

There are a lot of components to that, and I think a good coach, the decision making that they make within all that is what makes him a good coach. What information is important, where do we start, how do we get the most information across in the least amount of time and making sure that we get the information to the right people? Some coverage adjustment, the guard doesn't care about. He doesn't care about what coverage they're running. The receiver doesn't care if the nose is shaded or not shaded. But I'd say that's a very interesting part of game day from a coaching standpoint and one that's important, it's critical, and there are a lot of components to it.

Q: How different was Dick LeBeau's zone blitz when he came out with it?

BB: I'd say he definitely popularized it. When I was at the Giants, we ran some of that, but it was nowhere near to the degree that he ran it. We would just bring an extra guy at times based on formation or tendency or particular key, that kind of thing where we just add another guy in and still play zone behind it. When you have a 3-4 defense, the teams that ran the West Coast offense, they only had one protector on the strong side, so they get three guys out to the strong side and they would only have one blocker, so they would have to throw hot if you brought two guys over there.

But the zone blitz really killed that because there was a guy standing there to the guy that you were throwing hot to. I think once kind of everybody saw – and again the West Coast offense was pretty I'd say more prevalent and it didn't have as many variations as it has now both in the running game and the passing game. Back in the early to mid-90's with San Francisco and Mike Holmgren and all those guys, the zone blitz was a very effective way to play that offense because of the amount of three out strong, only one protector on the strong side, that if you brought two, they didn't have it. I think it really became popular there, and then that evolved into bringing two up the middle and two off the weak side and doing it out of sub and everything else. Dick was really the one who made it an entire package.

I would say at the Giants when we used it, it was more of either a very small situational call like short yardage or tight formations or that kind of thing or it was again something kind of specific. He made it just as a general defensive principle and developed it in a way that was very comprehensive on a number of levels —from a coverage standpoint, from attacking the pocket standpoint and also from a run defense perspective. Dick was really the guy that put that whole package together. Again I think there were maybe some random satellite elements of it here and there, and again I had some experience with that at the Giants, what we did, but nowhere near to the degree that he did it and popularized it.

Want more?

The Big Book of Belichick *is available via Amazon and Barnes & Noble paperback, Kindle, and on the Nook!*

OR go to AlexKirbyFootball.com to grab your copy today!

Printed in the USA
CPSIA information can be obtained
at www.ICGtesting.com
LVHW050245121223
766264LV00046B/1167